I know of no other book that zeros in on so many specific ways that God speaks to His children. This excellent book is first and foremost biblically based, but it's also been field tested by Larry Kreider's own e~~riences in listening to God over the years. It will not on^' God's will right now, but will serve as a r~^ or the future. *Joel Comiskey, Ph.D., a* ~~ia~~

Because of this book, many eai ~~.~o to the wonderful things the Father wants to tell F~~

Dave Witmer, pastor of Living Hope Community Church, Pennsylvania

Aren't there enough books about "Hearing God" already written? If you think so, you will change your mind as you hear Him speak to you personally through these pages! It's a powerful presentation of important insights often missed by others. Thanks, Larry, for the way you let the Father speak through you!
Ralph Neighbour, Touch Ministries, Texas

Hearing from God is the birthright of every believer, but all too often we become discouraged by the failure of mechanical or mystical formulas that are touted as new answers to an age-old yearning. Here is a refreshing guide to the multiplicity of ways God speaks to us, grounded firmly in the Word of God and filled with practical, spiritual insight. Thank you, Larry!
Richard Showalter, President, Eastern Mennonite Missions, Pennsylvania

Larry Kreider has blessed mankind with great insight on the variable ways God communicates His thoughts to mortal man on Earth. Every successful life and activity in the Bible was based on accurately hearing and obeying the directive voice of the Lord. This book contains the key to success for every person. All Christians will increase their relationship with God by understanding the 30 different ways that God communicates with mankind. This is one of the greatest books ever written on recognizing the voice of God through the many methods God uses. Thanks, Larry, for sharing this valuable knowledge you gained through much Bible studies, revelation knowledge and life experiences. *Dr. Bill Hamon, Apostle/Founder/Bishop of Christian International Ministries Network, Florida*

Larry Kreider has learned the secret to taking nations: draw near to the Father and do what He says. *Hearing God* is written from years of experience of shutting out the noise of the status quo and, as a son, learning to listen to and courageously obey the Father's voice. Our God has a passionate desire to speak to His children and partner with them in kingdom endeavors. This book will help many generations of sons and daughters hear the Father's voice, empowering them to fulfill their unique and supernatural destiny. This book is a call to join a loving God and live with Him outside of the box!
Jim Pesce, Executive Director of SYMBIOS Micro Communities International and Senior Elder of DOVE Harvest Church, Ontario

One of the questions most asked when releasing people into their destiny is "How do I know it is God's will?" This book will broaden for readers their perception of how God speaks and therefore enable them to be more confident in hearing. This is a timely book as God is stirring the hearts of a new generation.
Tony Fitzgerald, Apostolic Team leader for Church of the Nations

It is wonderful to recommend this book by Larry Kreider, a leader with great integrity. *Hearing God* is a comprehensive guide to hearing, yet not lengthy. As with so much that Larry does, it is amazingly biblically balanced. *Dr. Daniel Juster, Director Tikkun International, Maryland*

In an hour when the church is desperately needing clear teaching on practical, healthy ways to pursue the voice of God, Larry Kreider delivers. With ears pressing in to heaven and feet firmly planted on earth, Larry lets us know from a lifetime of experience and example the time-tested principles that help guide and shape the art of listening to God. For everyone who yearns for real-life answers to the quest to hear God's voice, you are holding them in your hand.
Robert Stearns, Executive Director, Eagles Wings, New York

Foreword

"How do I know God's will?" In over forty years of ministry this has been the foremost question I have been asked. The second most asked question often follows in the same conversation, "How do I hear God's voice?"

Throughout the chapters of this fast moving text Larry Kreider invites us to join in a spiritual journey that is marked by reliable signposts along the way. He also introduces us to some of the surprises that God may arrange to make our journey of faith very personal and less routine.

When an author firmly builds each of his or her points upon biblical truth, we feel secure with the foundation of the writer's thoughts. Biblical instruction, principles and examples give us strength to grow spiritually. Biblical soundness builds trust. Larry has chosen scriptural accounts that encourage us for the faith-stretching challenges of our day.

When an author is courageous with his or her thoughts, we are challenged to view life differently. In the pages that follow we will encounter some thoughts that go beyond conventional advice about hearing God's voice. In his encouraging style Larry invites us to discover God speaking to us in ways that others may have warned us against. I applaud his courage in bringing historically sound means of hearing God speak back into the mainstream of the contemporary church.

When an author is practical, the time we devote to thinking along with the writer is beneficial, and we are equipped to implement new understandings. Larry's life experience is generously sprinkled throughout his counsel to show that hearing God in everyday life is both practical and exciting.

Biblically sound, courageous, and practical . . . Turn the pages and see what I mean.

Keith E. Yoder
Teaching The Word Ministries
Leola, Pennsylvania

Introduction

If there is one thing I have learned over the years, it is that God is a God of surprises. We can never limit God in any way, including the way He will speak to us. He created us to communicate with Him and He longs for those times. What we'll explore in this book is that we can expect God to speak, but it may be in unexpected ways.

It would be easy if we could just dial a number on a spiritual cell phone and hear the reassuring voice of God answering, "Hello, this is God speaking!" Yet, in reality, He is speaking to us every day in ways we may often miss. The Bible says, "For God does speak—now one way, now another—though man may not perceive it."[1]

The Bible gives us many clues to hearing God's voice. We'll discover that our ears must be tuned to hear Him. The Lord has an enormous range of options for speaking to us. He may use the inner witness of the Holy Spirit, His Word, prayer, circumstances or other people. The Lord may speak to us in dreams, visions or even by His audible voice; however, don't expect God's audible voice to be the common way He will speak! God's voice often blends into a melodic harmony to which we have to tune in.

Jesus promised that if we listen to Him closely, we will receive more and more from Him. He said, "Be careful what you are hearing. The measure you give will be the measure that comes back to you, and more will be given to you who hear."[2]

When we take the time to listen carefully, we can know the difference between His voice and other voices that do not match the character of God, His nature and the history of how He has led others before us. Jesus urges us to learn to listen like sheep, "They will never follow a stranger, but will run away from him because they do not know the voice of strangers or recognize their call."[3]

As His children, His voice becomes familiar to us as we develop a relationship with Him. If you do not have a relationship with God through Jesus Christ, turn now to page 214 to see how Jesus came to reconcile you to God.[4] The Bible says that when we accept Jesus as our Lord and Savior, we are given a deposit of the Holy Spirit as a promise of what is yet to come.[5] With the presence of the Holy Spirit within, we receive the help we need to pray and discern what our heavenly Father is saying to us.[6]

Although we'll consider thirty different ways the Lord speaks to us in this book, it is not the final word on how He will choose to communicate. God is sovereign. He speaks in different ways at different times. Our faith must always be in God and not in a certain method.

Among the myriad of ways God speaks, we may not consider some to be particularly spiritual. For example, this book has a chapter on hearing God speak through common sense. If you want to buy a new house and cannot afford it, God is probably telling you to wait until He provides the money for you.

I believe even those who have experienced divine intervention or amazing angelic visitations will tell you that most often the Lord speaks through the Word of God, the peace of God, circumstances, His still small voice, other Christians, and through common sense wisdom.

Even with that said, our God is so infinitely amazing and wise and creative that He does not limit Himself to speaking in the same ways all of the time. God thinks outside the box! He is a little unpredictable, not unlike Aslan the lion in *The Chronicles of Narnia*, "One day you'll see him and another you won't. He doesn't like being tied down—and of course he has other countries to attend to. It's quite all right. He'll often drop in. Only you mustn't press him. He's wild, you know. Not like a *tame* lion."[7]

If you want to hear from God, you must trust Him even if you can't use one safe method or formula to hear from Him. Allow God to surprise you! Trust Him to speak to you. Cultivate your friendship with God. You are in a lifetime walk with the Creator of the universe, and hearing His voice is a skill to be learned over time.

Hearing God
30 ways in 30 days

How to use this book

This book has one objective—to help you realize you can hear God's voice. Within its 30 chapters, *Hearing God* includes 30 ways that God communicates. Whether you are an individual reading this book for personal reflection or working through this book with a friend, church or a group study, expect God to speak to you, even in unexpected ways.

Suggested study formats
Personal devotional Take the next 30 days, reading a chapter each day, utilizing the questions to apply what you have learned.

Group study Study each chapter in a small group setting. Discuss the questions at the end of each chapter.

Mentoring relationship Take another person through the book as a one-on-one discipling tool.

Church course Pastors may use this book as a resource for teaching or preaching. One church or multiple churches could join together for an extended 30-day course.

Go ahead, turn the page and get started!

The Lord wants us to take the time to listen as we open our hearts to hear. He wants us to become increasingly familiar with His voice as our relationship deepens with Him. The more often we meet with God in prayer and talk to Him, the clearer His voice becomes.

The Bible instructs us to make a concerted effort to meet with the Lord, thereby placing ourselves in a position to hear from Him. "Then you will call upon me and come and pray to me, and I will listen to you. You will seek me and find me when you seek me with all your heart."[4] We can't make demands on God, but we can ask, seek and knock, and the Bible promises that God will open the door.[5] God will reveal Himself to those who humbly seek Him.

God wants us to acknowledge Him in our lives.[6] If we acknowledge a friend, we talk to him, express our appreciation for him, and recognize his presence in our lives.

Imagine your friends not acknowledging your presence when you are together. You try to talk to them, and they completely ignore you. In fact, they talk right over you as if you were not even there. That is how we treat the Lord if we are not acknowledging Him moment by moment in our lives. If we are not recognizing God's presence in our daily lives, it is little wonder we are having trouble hearing from Him.

Tune in

The truth is, even when we diligently seek God for an answer, we sometimes find ourselves struggling to hear. We really want to do what the Lord wants us to do. We know that we serve a living God who speaks to us, and yet we struggle with the fact that we do not hear as clearly as we would like.

Other times we think we have heard the Lord's voice and respond to it, only to find out that we were wrong. Instead of pressing in to find out why we "missed it," we hesitate to step out in faith the next time.

Frequently it may seem as if we are trying to tune in to a weak radio signal with a lot of static. That's why I wrote this book. I want you to discover that God wants to speak to you even more than your desire to hear from Him, and He has many different ways to communicate with you. We cannot put Him in a box.

Although we may wish that God would send a ten foot angel dressed in white so we have no doubt it is His voice we are hearing, I believe He often teaches us through our stumbling attempts of trial and error.

Selective hearing?

Even Jesus' disciples did not always recognize His voice. When Jesus joined two of His disciples on the road to Emmaus and began to talk to them, they didn't recognize Him even though they had walked with him, talked with Him and eaten meals with Him for the past three years.[7] Perhaps they were so immersed in the details of the dark events of the past few days that they couldn't hear clearly.

I think there is a good chance, however, that they did not see Jesus because they simply did not expect to see Jesus. He appeared to them in an unfamiliar form, at an unexpected time, and their ears remained closed.

Before we criticize these disciples, we must ask ourselves, "How often do we experience the same loss of hearing today?" Could it be that the Lord sometimes speaks to us in ways that are unfamiliar to us, and we don't recognize His voice? We lament that we can't hear Him speak, but in reality He has been speaking all along. Could it be that our understanding of hearing His voice is limited? Maybe we have preconceived ideas how God will speak or not speak to us, and they limit us in hearing from God when He speaks.

I'm convinced we should not get too selective about the method in which the Lord speaks to us. Instead, we should stay open for the Lord to speak to us any way He desires. I spend

Hearing God

Just like Samuel, you too have to learn to discern if you are hearing the Lord's voice or another voice. Don't worry if you feel like a modern-day Samuel who does not recognize God's voice right away; you will learn in time! Listening takes time and requires discernment.

One time I was driving down a rural road when I passed a hitchhiker. I sensed a voice telling me to go back and pick him up. I thought the Lord wanted me to share my faith with him. When I turned around, he was nowhere in sight. I was confused. I thought the Lord had spoken to me; but I missed it! This was just a part of the Lord's training process for me to learn to hear His voice clearly.

Discernment comes with practice

The writer of Hebrews tells us that we can train ourselves to recognize the voice of God above all the various other voices. "Solid food is for mature people who have been trained to know right from wrong."[8] It is by practicing that we are able to discern whether what we hear is of God, our own voice, or the devil.

A basketball player was asked how he scored the game-point 3-pointer under incredible pressure and said, "That's why I've practiced 3-pointers every day for years." Through practice he trained his body to shoot in an almost automatic fashion. Discernment comes with practice. You have to constantly evaluate beliefs, feelings, other people, the media and your own inner life in light of God's Word. Over time, you train your senses to do it almost by reflex.

Ask God to communicate to you during your prayer times with Him and all throughout the day. You will learn more and more to discern the difference between your voice, others' voices, the voice of the enemy, and the voice of the Holy Spirit. You will learn how to hear the voice of God and obey Him. Remember, listening is an art.

In the next chapter, we will start with the first and the most important way of hearing God speak—*through His written Word, the*

Bible. This is the purest and surest way that God speaks to us. Jesus said, "If you continue in My Word, then you are truly disciples of Mine; and you will know the truth, and the truth will make you free."⁹ We will never go off track if we obey the Word of God.

Hearing the Right Voice

Verse to remember "We demolish arguments and every pretension that sets itself up against the knowledge of God, and we take captive every thought to make it obedient to Christ" (2 Corinthians 10:5-6).

Apply what you've learned
1. Describe a time you knew it was not God's voice but another voice you were hearing.
2. How have you ever confused your own desires with the voice of the Lord? How did you finally know it was happening?
3. How does discerning God's voice come with practice?

PART II
30 of the many ways God speaks

Chapter Three

God speaks through

The Bible

God has spoken and continues to speak through His Word, the Bible. It must be the first and last word in your life; it is your ultimate authority, the measuring stick that you can use to gauge your life.

The Holy Bible is an amazing book. It is the most influential book in all history—the world's all-time best seller. In every generation since it was written, it has been looked at as a source of understanding for the world we live in and the reason for our existence. We should read it with the expectation that God will speak to us here and now through its words. If we listen, we can hear God's voice addressing us through the Bible.

The Scriptures are filled with life values, stories of God's mercy toward mankind and parables packed with important truths for every individual, regardless of culture or background. It is written as a personal love letter to each of us. God speaks to us and directs us, molding us into vessels for His purposes and plans by His written Word. He sets the direction for our lives so we can know where we are going.

God speaks to you directly through the Bible.

The Bible is the written, divine expression or revelation of God to humanity. In the Greek, there are two words that describe God's Word—*logos* and *rhema*. *Logos* is the truth spoken or revealed (established), and *rhema* is the truth speaking and communicating personally (illuminating our lives). God can take the *logos* Word and make it *rhema* to you personally.

For example, your name doesn't appear on the pages of the Bible, but God can speak to you personally at any time. Sometimes a scripture will seem to "jump out at you"; it comes alive in a particular way. That is when the *logos* becomes a specific *rhema* to you. It only becomes alive when you apply it to your life. The Bible would be a lifeless history book without this kind of personal revelation

The *rhema* Word of the Lord is the "voice" of the tried-and-proven established Word of God. The *rhema* Word is made alive as though God just spoke it into your ears. His *rhema* Word will always be supported in the established truth revealed in the *logos* Word of God. Without *logos* there would be no *rhema*.

God will never contradict the Bible

If you want to hear God's voice, you must study the Bible. Of all the other ways that God may speak to you, He will never contradict His written Word in the Bible. His *logos* applies for every situation in life. His written Word does not change. You can trust it for final authority. Reject anything that contradicts the written Bible.

When God speaks to us about something that is not directly addressed in the Bible, it will always be in agreement with the Bible. For example, the Bible doesn't tell us where to work or where to live or whom to marry, but God will speak His *rhema* Word to us about these things if we seek Him. The Bible confirms whether what we think is the *rhema* Word of the Lord really is His voice.

Jesus reveals to us that the words He has spoken to us are spirit and life.[1] God's Word divides between truth and deception. If God has truly spoken to us, it will *always* line up with the Bible. Osama bin Laden, the Islamic fundamentalist who led a terrorist attack on America, believed he heard from God; but he and his philosophies are miles apart from the scriptures, and he is living in utter deception.

When Jesus was tempted by the devil, He made it clear that God's Word is what gives us life and strength. We can use food or other material goods, but our trust must be in spiritual things—God's Word. "Man does not live on bread alone, but on every word that comes from the mouth of God."[2] The Bible contains the food that our souls require. We must feed on God's written Word for spiritual health. We can always trust the Bible.

The Bible is our final authority. It tells us, "Study and be eager and do your utmost to present yourself to God approved, a workman who has no cause to be ashamed, correctly analyzing and accurately dividing the Word of Truth."[3]

The Bible gives us direct guidance on many issues of life. For example, should a believer in Christ marry an unsaved person? God's written Word gives us a clear answer when it tells us to not be unequally joined together with an unbeliever.[4] If we do not know what the Bible says, we can be easily deceived into thinking that whatever we are feeling is the Lord leading us. This is very dangerous. This is why we must study the scriptures.

We can hear God through Bible teachers who preach the Word

Sit under the teaching of those who are seasoned Bible teachers because they are mouthpieces of the Lord. They can help to clarify things you are not sure about or do not understand in the Bible. Teachers long to communicate what God is saying so that you can hear God for yourself. Teachers know it is not their task to give their own opinions or ideas but to be facilitators of what God is saying through the Bible. They reveal that God's Word is truth and encourage you to check out this truth in the Bible.

Soak in God's Word

Saturate yourself with the Word of God. Most people eat three meals a day. How many meals of God's Word do we devour? There are many ways to saturate ourselves with the Bible. We can read through it chapters at a time or use a Greek dictionary to thoroughly study parts of it. Other times we can meditate on the four gospels or the epistles (the letters written by Paul). We may want to read through the Psalms for months at a time. We can read one chapter of Proverbs a day for a complete month because there are 31 chapters. Memorizing God's Word allows us to "hide" it in our hearts. Sometimes we will want to read and reread one verse over and over and meditate on it.

My friend Steve says that if he needs a word from the Lord, he searches the Bible until God shows him and confirms something in his spirit. He has come to realize that God's written word will never take him off course.

We must have a full reservoir of the Word of God to draw from so we are not deceived by the enemy. Any dream, prophecy, vision or audible voice that does not line up with God's written Word is not the voice of God. Scripture is given as a standard so that we will never get off track. God's Word is described this way: "All Scripture is God-breathed and is useful for teaching, rebuking, correcting and training in righteousness, so that the man of God may be thoroughly equipped for every good work."[5]

Obedience required

A man asked me once if I could give my "stamp of approval" on his decision to divorce his Christian wife and marry another woman in the church whom he felt could be more compatible with him in his ministry. I told him that no matter how right it felt to him, his plan was in direct disobedience to the Lord. How did I know? The Scripture clearly say that he would be committing adultery.[6] God's Word requires obedience whether we feel like doing it or not.

In his book *In Pursuit of Obedience*, Steve Prokopchak challenges us to love God enough to obey Him:

> Even though our God—full of love, compassion, and
> understanding—wants us to enjoy life to its fullest,
> He has always had boundaries for His people....When
> I set a limit for one of my children, it is because I
> love him and have his best interests in mind....Do you
> love God enough to obey Him when the limit is
> "uncomfortable" for you?[7]

God sets limits for us because He loves us. If we want to mature in our Christian lives, we must renew our minds with God's Word so we know God's boundaries and can distinguish between right and wrong.

Correctly interpreting the Bible for your life

God's Word never changes. Many times, however, the area in which we need guidance is not specifically addressed in the scriptures. We may need to know the answers for some of the following questions. What is the Lord's plan for my career? Whom should I marry? Do I need to consider further training? Where should I live? Should I buy a house or rent? Should I go to college? With which group of believers has the Lord called me to serve? This is the time to learn to listen to the voice of the Holy Spirit speaking to our spirits, confirmed by His written Word.

It is extremely important to correctly interpret the original intent of what we read in the Bible so we can apply God's Word intelligently to our contemporary situation. When we read the Bible, we need to listen to the voice of God coming through His Word, and avoid taking scripture out of context or misusing it for our own interpretations. The Bible never contradicts itself, but sometimes can be taken out of context. For example, if we take no regard for context, Paul seems to contradict himself by saying at one place that we are not saved by works[8] and in another place that we are to work out our salvation.[9] Scripture, read in context, will reconcile these two seemingly opposing verses. According to one biblical teacher we should always read the Bible in light of the whole message God wants to convey to us:

> When Paul wrote the epistles, he wrote a coherent, holistic message. He never intended for someone a couple millennia later to rip verses out of their context and wield them any way they so chose! Certainly we have a right to quote verses of scripture; but we do not have a right to ignore the context, or to make them say what the language cannot say. Otherwise, someone could come along and say "Judas hanged himself"; "Go and do likewise"! Hence, one reason for the abuse of scripture is due to a lack of respect for the Bible as a divine and human work. In this approach it becomes a magical incantation book—almost a book of unconnected fortune cookie sayings![10]

If some scriptures are hard to understand, we must do our homework and study the meaning and context of the passage. Since our modern culture is different from that of Bible times, we often have a cultural gap that needs interpretation. We can ask a seasoned believer who has studied biblical principles of interpretation to help us understand what the Lord is saying through a scripture that doesn't make sense to us.

Revelation must agree with the Bible

If anyone claims to have supernatural revelation from God, it must agree with the Word of God.[11] The Mormon cult was started by Joseph Smith, a man who claimed he had a visitation from an angel. We know this was a fallen angel or demonic spiritual being, because the message did not coincide with the written Word of God. It was a perversion of the true gospel.

Paul, the apostle, urges the Galatian believers not to be persuaded by false teachers. "I am astonished that you are so quickly deserting the one who called you by the grace of Christ and are turning to a different gospel—which is really no gospel at all. Evidently some people are throwing you into confusion and are trying to pervert the gospel of Christ. But even if we or an angel from heaven should preach a gospel other than the one we preached to you, let him be eternally condemned!"[12] Just because someone quotes scripture does not mean that they necessarily have God's intentions in mind.

Remember, the Bible says Satan comes to us like an angel of light.[13] In order not to be deceived, we should be like the Bereans who checked whether the Christian interpretation Paul put on the Old Testament scriptures was the true one.[14] They checked everything by the written Word of God, and we should too. The written Word of God is our standard to be sure that the revelation we are receiving is in line with the perfect will of God. We know the Holy Spirit wrote the scriptures, so he will not speak anything to us that disagrees with the scriptures.

God reveals His will through the Bible

Stephanie was single for a large part of her young adulthood. After dating one particular young man for several months, they decided to stop seeing each other because they were unsure about the direction their relationship should go.

Stephanie asked the Lord if she should move on from the relationship or fast and pray over it for further revelation. She recalls, "A short time later I came across this verse, 'But the time will come when the bridegroom will be taken from them; in those days they will fast.'"[15] Through this verse in the Word speaking to her spirit, Stephanie felt that the Lord was challenging her to pray and fast because there was possibility in the relationship. And her bridegroom did return! They were married a year and half later. God's written Word will speak directly to our dilemmas, revealing the direction we should go.

The Bible says, "For the word of God is living and active. Sharper than any double-edged sword, it penetrates even to dividing soul and spirit, joints and marrow; it judges the thoughts and attitudes of the heart."[16] God speaks to us through our minds and our spirits and reveals His purposes to us.

We live in a real world with real problems, and we need real answers. The answers are found in God's Word and are revealed to us by His Holy Spirit. We must spend time alone with God and His Word. God's written Word tells us,

> My son, attend to my words; consent and submit to my sayings. Let them not depart from your sight, keep them in the center of your heart, for they are life to those who find them.[17]

God's written Word will steer you in the right direction as you make it the first and last word in your life.

You can hear God through the Bible

Verse to remember "The words I have spoken to you are spirit and they are life" (John 6:63).

Apply what you've learned
1. How is the Bible a measuring stick for you to use to gauge your life?
2. Explain the difference between God's *rhema* word and *logos* word.
3. How did you interpret the Bible when it did not specifically address the area in which you needed guidance?
4. How have you personally heard God speak to you through the Bible?

Chapter Four

God speaks through
His Peace

God's peace is a lighthouse to guide you in the right direction.

I learned a principle from a man of God many years ago that has helped to steer me in the right direction as I have attempted to hear God's voice. It is a story of three lighthouses. Three lighthouses were built in formation to warn ships of the monstrous rocks below the surface of the water as they sailed into a particular harbor. To avoid getting snagged on these huge rocks, the captain had to be sure that the three lighthouses were perfectly aligned as he guided his ship into the harbor. If the captain could see two or three lighthouses at the same time, he knew he was in the danger zone.

In order to avoid shipwreck in our lives, we need to be sure that three different "lighthouses" are aligned before we begin to move in a new direction. These lighthouses are the Word of God, peace and circumstances.

Peace is a confirmation you are hearing from God.

In the previous chapter, we already talked about the importance of hearing God speak to us through the Bible. If we want to hear from the Lord and be successful in our Christian lives, we must be faithful to God's Word. "Do not let this Book of the Law depart from your mouth; meditate on it day and night, so that you may be careful to do everything written in it. Then you will be prosperous and successful."[1] When we ignore the Bible, it takes its eventual toll on our lives and causes us spiritual shipwreck.

God's peace is a vital ingredient for hearing from Him

Along with hearing God speak to us through the Bible, a second significant lighthouse to align is the lighthouse of peace. Jesus spoke of the kind of peace He offers when He said, "Peace I leave with you; my peace I give you. I do not give to you as the world gives. Do not let your hearts be troubled and do not be afraid." [2]

When you really believe and trust, having confidence in God, you will not have worry or fear in your heart. Peace is the result of trusting completely. Inner peace is hard to define, but the Bible says it surpasses human comprehension.[3] As you learn to hear the voice of God, a distinct calmness fills your heart.

Inner peace comes from an unwavering trust in Jesus. When our trust is in Jesus, who is our only true source of peace, He dispels the fears that grip us in an uncertain world and in the midst of our own faults and failures. It is only through faith in Jesus and in the work that He has already done on the cross that we can *know* peace.

Let peace rule in your heart

The Bible says, "Let the peace of Christ rule in your hearts, since as members of one body you were called to peace. And be thankful."[4] The word "rule" literally means *to be an umpire*. In other words, the peace of God in our hearts is an umpire to alert us as to whether or not we should make a certain decision.

A lack of peace may be the Holy Spirit warning us that we should not go ahead in a particular direction in our lives. We should not make decisions if our hearts are unsettled. The peace of God in our hearts will lead us to making the right decisions.

A man was offered a job by a large company where he would make much more money than he ever made in his life. As he considered the offer, he thought of all the wonderful philanthropic things he could do with the extra money: use it to help friends, give to the poor, help the homeless. He did not have peace from God about taking the job, however, so he turned it down.

The president of the company thought he was crazy, as did some friends. It seemed like a once-in-a-lifetime opportunity; but he could not take it without the blessing of God. A short time later it was discovered that the president of the company committed many illegal dealings, and the whole company was in trouble. If he had taken the job, he might have been implicated just because he worked there. At the very least, he would have had to choose between being honest and keeping the job. God kept this man from getting involved in a very unpleasant situation.

Several years ago a friend told me he wanted to give me his car as a gift. It was a beautiful car; but my wife LaVerne and I did not have the peace of God in our hearts to receive it. So we graciously declined. Some time later, the Lord provided our family with a customized van, and this time we had the peace to receive it from the benefactor. It was the perfect vehicle for our growing family.

I speak at a church in a city somewhere in the world almost every weekend. How do I know which invitations to take and which ones to decline? I often depend on the peace of God. When I am asked to speak and do not have the peace of God in my spirit, I decline. I have learned over the years it always pays to obey the peace that God places in my heart.

Recently I had the privilege of investing some money into a business that paid great dividends. I was ready to reinvest the money into the same company again; but my wife LaVerne did not have peace about it. I have learned to listen to what the Lord speaks to my wife, so I did not invest. We later discovered the company was involved in massive financial difficulties, and had I invested money into it, I would have lost every cent I put in. We followed our *lack of peace* and the Lord used it to protect us.

I was talking to a friend recently who is struggling with God's will regarding which church to attend in his community. I simply encouraged him to follow the peace of God because the Bible says, "And the peace of God, which transcends all understanding, will guard your hearts and your minds in Christ Jesus."[5]

Remember, when the deceiver speaks to us, he cannot give true peace. When we try to solve things with our own reasoning, we cannot get true peace in our spirits. You don't have to explain to other people why you don't have peace about a certain thing; sometimes you won't even know why yourself.

Even when you believe God has spoken, you should wait until peace fills your heart to do what you believe He has instructed you. In this way, you are assured that your timing is right. Peace is a confirmation that you are hearing from the Lord. If I am shopping with my wife, we don't buy something if we don't have peace about it. If we are working on a particular project and start to feel uneasy about it, we are not acting from faith if we continue to push on without examining why peace has dissipated.

Peace is closely tied to "conviction," which we will examine in a later chapter. I like the way this teacher of the Word shows its connection:

> If we don't feel right about something like littering,
> we shouldn't just go ahead and do it anyway. It
> doesn't work to use the excuse that everyone else does
> what we're convicted not to do. Many of God's
> people are powerless because they continually do
> things their conscience tells them not to do. When we
> don't pay heed to our conscience, we lose our peace.
> The Word teaches us to be true to our convictions; if
> we do something we feel uneasy about, we stand
> condemned because we are not acting from faith (see
> Romans 14:23).[6]

God Speaks Through His Peace   43

We should never act without peace; it is a vital ingredient to hearing God's voice. Peace is an "internal confirmation" that the action being taken is approved of by God. Obeying the peace of God in our hearts allows us to carry on with a sense of His acceptance and favor in our lives.

Along with the previous "lighthouses" of *God's Word* and *God's peace*, a third spiritual lighthouse that needs to line up is the lighthouse of *circumstances* (open doors) that the Lord places before us. We will look further at how God uses circumstances to speak to us in the next chapter.

You can hear God through His peace

Verse to remember: "Let the peace of Christ rule in your hearts, since as members of one body you were called to peace..." (Colossians 3:15).

Apply what you've learned:

1. Think of a time your heart was unsettled and you did not make a decision because you did not have a peace about it. Was it God speaking?
2. Can you describe the inner peace that comes from trusting Jesus?
3. How does "peace" and "conviction" go hand-in-hand when it comes to hearing from God?
4. Describe a time you felt the peace of God and made a decision in light of it.

Chapter Five

God speaks through
Circumstances

God speaks to us through opening and closing doors of circumstances.

I was in Nairobi, Kenya, a few years ago when terrorists bombed the US Embassy, killing nearly one thousand people. That morning, Diane Omondi, the wife of the pastor who was sponsoring the leadership training at which I was teaching, planned to go to the embassy to help process a visa for a friend. Through a set of circumstances at the last minute, it did not work out for her to go.

Had she gone, Diane could have been in the US Embassy when the bomb exploded. In this instance, the Lord used a "closed door" circumstance to protect one of His children. The Bible says that God can open a door or close it at will, "These are the words of the Holy One, the True One, He Who has the key of David, Who opens and no one shall shut, Who shuts and no one shall open."[1]

Paul saw God open a door of opportunity for him and believed it was the Lord directing him through the providential circumstances. "After I go through Macedonia, I will come to you...I hope to spend some time with you, if the

> **Open and closed doors of circumstances help you to hear from God.**

Lord permits. But I will stay on at Ephesus until Pentecost, because a great door for effective work has opened to me, and there are many who oppose me."[2]

The Lord clearly opened up a door for Paul in Ephesus. The circumstances lined up with the Word of God and with the peace of God, and although Paul faced many adversaries, he knew that the Lord wanted him to stay in Ephesus.

We must be aware that not every open door means we should go running through it. The key to walking through an open door is to know without a doubt that *the Lord* has opened it. The Holy Spirit must be speaking to us before we make a move to walk in a new direction.

Circumstances that seemingly reveal open doors may not necessarily be the Lord speaking to us to move in a particular direction. Focusing only on the circumstances can be misleading. For example, a college student may receive a large scholarship to attend a particular university, but he must know that God is in it or he may make the wrong choice just because the circumstances are favorable.

Before we walk through an open door, we must believe that it is God who is speaking to us within the circumstances, have the peace of God about it and know it does not conflict with God's Word.

Timing

Sometimes we can be so sure that something is God's will, but God does not open up the doors for us because it is not the right timing. If you feel this way, it is best to let the desire die. If it is really from God, He will resurrect it (bring it back to life) in the future when the timing is right.

We have counseled countless young men and women who were sure the Lord had shown them whom they should marry, but the other person wasn't getting the same message. Our advice is to let the desire die for now, and if the Lord has really spoken it to you, it will happen sometime in the future. We all hear from

God "in part"[3] and we must recognize that we do not always hear clearly.

If you believe the Lord wants you to buy a certain house or car, and it is not available, either you have missed the timing or it is not the Lord's answer for you. Timing is so important.

Brian was friends with a young woman and felt called to marry her. She, however, was preparing to go on a church planting team to another nation. It was apparent to Brian the timing was not right, so he waited for a year and a half until Janet returned. After her return from missionary service, he asked her to marry him, and she said "yes." Although God spoke to Brian much earlier about marrying Janet, the timing had to be right.

You may have the right direction from the Lord, but the wrong timing as you try to fulfill it. Moses had the right vision from the Lord (deliver the Lord's people from the slavery of the Egyptians). The only problem was that he initially missed the timing of God (by forty years!) when he killed an Egyptian.

A friend recently shared how God works through circumstances and timing in his marriage relationship to help them make godly decisions. He told me that he often gets new vision and plans from God for their lives and is ready to move on that vision because he believes God is opening the door of circumstances. His wife, on the other hand, does not always immediately see the open door. When she does, the timing has always been correct. Consequently, he has learned over many years of marriage that he most often hears God's voice first in the open door, but it is his wife who hears the timing. Together, as one, they can then hear God to make the right decision.

Doors will open

Someone may feel called to start a business or be a missionary, and the plan is a genuine vision from the Lord. Often the problem comes when they jump into it too fast. When the Lord is in it, the circumstances will work out. The third lighthouse will line up.

God Speaks Through Circumstances

Jeremiah gives an interesting account of heeding the voice of the Lord through circumstances.

> Then this message from the Lord came to Jeremiah: "Your cousin Hanamel (son of Shallum) will soon arrive to ask you to buy the farm he owns in Anathoth, for by law you have a chance to buy before it is offered to anyone else." So, Hanamel came, as the Lord had said he would, and visited me in the prison. "Buy my field in Anathoth, in the land of Benjamin," he said, "for the law gives you the first right to purchase it." Then I knew for sure that the message I had heard was really from the Lord.[4]

After the circumstances lined up, Jeremiah knew that the message was a sure word from the Lord. If the Lord is asking you to do something, He will make it clear. You can trust Him.

If we are not sure about the open doors, we can trust God to speak within the circumstances in which we currently find ourselves. Recently I talked to two young men who are in high school. They were wondering what the Lord was saying to them and how He could use them. They were simply high school students attempting to make the best of every opportunity God gave them. Then they started to realize that God had them in school for a reason. That was what God wanted to speak to them—to be used exactly where they were. They focused on school in a new way, and guess what God showed them to do? These two young men began inviting their friends from school to their church every week. Many responded. School was the circumstance providing their open doors for ministry.

In Acts 27, Paul was shipwrecked on the island of Malta. This shipwreck circumstance led to Paul's three month stay on the island resulting in many of the people opening up to the gospel.

During 2003, I thought the Lord could be leading me to go to the nation of Korea. It had been more than a dozen years since I was there last, and I wanted to be sure about the timing of the trip. I prayed and asked the Lord to provide the finances for me to go if it was His will. The money never came in to make it possible, so I concluded that I was not to go. This was confirmed as I got closer to the originally planned date.

Instead, God opened doors for me to spend time with my daughter in California and with Christian leaders in New Zealand. Without a doubt, I knew this was the best plan for me at this time. God spoke through my circumstances.

Recently, I felt a burden to go to Australia to pray for the nation. I left it in the Lord's hands, and He opened the doors in a way I did not expect. I was scheduled to fly to New Zealand through Los Angeles, but since there were forest fires at that time in Los Angeles, I knew I would miss my flight because of the delays. I called the airline the night before I was to leave and they informed me that due to forest fires, the only way to go to New Zealand was through Australia, and they would send me via that route at no extra cost!

I was able to spend a few hours in Australia to pray for the nation before going to New Zealand. Using my circumstances, God opened the door in a way that was totally unexpected to me. Sometimes the interruptions in life are in reality "divine interruptions."

Pray for circumstances to change

If we believe God wants us to move ahead in a certain direction but the circumstances do not match God's revealed will, He may be calling us to prayer, spiritual warfare and action to see the circumstance change. In 1 Kings 18, God showed Elijah that He would send rain to end a drought. Elijah prayed for the rain, but it did not come. Seven times he sent his servant to look at the sky to see if rain clouds were forming. No rain! Elijah was persistent in his prayer. Rather than get discouraged, he simply kept on praying until he saw evidence of the answer to his prayer. Elijah prayed earnestly because he wanted to participate in the means by which God achieves His ends. He believed God would send rain because God had promised it, but he had to keep praying until the circumstances changed. The circumstances did change. It rained just as God said it would, but only after Elijah resolutely prayed and persevered for the circumstances to change.

Step out

Bible teacher Joyce Meyer once said, "Sometimes the only way to discover God's will is to practice what I call 'stepping out and finding out.' If I have prayed about a situation and don't seem to know what I should do, I take a step of faith...trusting Him is like standing before the automatic door to a supermarket. We can stand and look at the door all day, but it won't open until we take a step forward and trigger the mechanism that opens the door. There are times in life when we must take a step forward in order to find out, one way or the other, what we should do. Some doors will never open unless we take a step toward them."[5]

In the book of Acts and in 1 Corinthians 16, Paul, Silas, and Barnabas did not sit and wait for an angel to appear or a vision to be given to them while praying for direction. They took steps in the direction they felt were correct. Many times God did open the door, but there were times when He closed the door. This did not discourage them. They were not afraid of "missing God." They were men of faith and action. They also knew to back off quickly when it became evident that God was not permitting them to follow their plan.

Today, we too can hear God's voice through circumstances as He opens and closes doors of opportunity. The key is to always be led by the Holy Spirit, not by the circumstances themselves. He may capture our attention by a combination of factors that include open door circumstances and a word from a friend. Others times He could speak through circumstances that lead us to scripture that confirms the circumstances. God speaks to our individual need. We will sense when He has spoken.

Chapter Seven

God speaks through
People

There is safety in a multitude of counselors.

I have often heard the Lord speak to me through the counsel of others; and more times than I can count, the Lord used my wife to speak something that God wanted to say to me. God wants us to pay attention to godly people who have consistently listened to Him and obeyed Him. These wise counselors have become familiar with God's voice and can give us godly insights that will aid us in making proper decisions.

Proverbs discloses the benefits of listening to godly counselors for advice, "Where there is no counsel, the people fall; but in the multitude of counselors there is safety."[1] God often uses the counsel of other believers to clarify ambiguous areas or to give us the assurance that we are truly hearing from Him. These people speak "a word in due season" to help us to discern God's voice. Sometimes they can give us a word of advice that confirms what we already feel in our own spirit.

My friend Beth recalls a time God spoke to her through another person who gave her much needed godly counsel. Beth is a person who loves to give to others and often gets ideas of gifts and creative things to do for people. For a period of time, however, she started to

Wise counselors give insights to help us hear from God.

feel that her ideas were just too expensive and took too much time to implement. Some time later, during a group prayer time, a man told Beth a story he sensed was from the Lord. He told the Bible story of the woman pouring out the expensive perfume on Jesus' feet. Others complained about the wasted resource. Beth immediately knew God truly was challenging her to continue to give to others as part of her giving to Him. It was worth the time and cost, just as Jesus was worth it. Beth was grateful that someone had heard from God and challenged her to do what she knew deep inside God had called her to do. God had spoken to her through another person.

We need each other

I think the reason God uses others to help us hear His voice is to remind us that we are not self-sufficient. God placed us on earth to interact with others and give up our self-centeredness and independence so we can become interdependent. We need each other.

Soon after a young woman I know turned 30, she asked the Lord if she was ever going to get married or if she should prepare for a lifetime of singleness. Several days after she asked this question, someone she knew and trusted came to her and said, "I feel impressed by the Holy Spirit to tell you that God has a special person just for you!" Because this was a question she had privately asked God, the young woman really hadn't expected God to speak through another person like this. She was unexpectedly surprised and encouraged all at the same time. And God did bring someone into her life a few years later.

The Bible says it is a privilege and a joy to be able to hear from God and pass that guidance on to another. "A man finds joy in giving an apt reply—and how good is a timely word!"[2] I was talking recently to a friend in Canada, and he asked me for advice on decisions he was making for his future. I gave him the guidance I felt the Lord was giving to me for him. He mentioned it was the same advice a friend from Uzbekistan gave him earlier that day. In this case, the same word was confirmed by two people, and my friend joyfully received it as a word from God.

Paul, the apostle, believed in the importance of getting a confirmation of two or three people. "Every matter must be established by the testimony of two or three witnesses."[3] If God has spoken something to you, He will usually confirm it through another.

The scriptures tell us there is power in agreement. "Again, I tell you that if two of you on earth agree about anything you ask for, it will be done for you by my Father in heaven. For where two or three come together in my name, there am I with them."[4] God often speaks to us through agreement with others.

I was in a strategic planning meeting recently, and within a few minutes three different men felt the same impression of the Lord about a fairly obscure Bible story. The Lord used this story to give us direction for the future.

Sometimes people tell me, "God spoke to me, and I am not accountable to anyone, just God." People who rarely ask for or take advice are usually dealing with pride in their lives. Pride can keep us from accepting counsel from others.

Our culture may tell us to stand on our own two feet because we don't need anyone to help us make decisions. A proud person thinks seeking advice is a sign of weakness; however, as a community of believers in Jesus, we were designed for interdependence. God speaks through other believers to benefit every member in the body of Christ.

Preachers help people hear God

A common way God speaks to us is through one of His servants who is preaching under the guidance of the Holy Spirit. Biblical preachers believe God is speaking, through His Word and His Spirit and through *them*, as they are faithful to the task of preaching God's Word.

I have often heard God speak to my spirit while listening to a preacher or teacher expounding God's Word, and it became alive to me at that moment. Preachers help us hear what God is saying.

Romans 10 shows Paul's concern for those who cannot call on the name of the Lord because no one has told them of Him:

> How, then, can they call on the one they have not believed in? And how can they believe in the one of whom they have not heard? And how can they hear without someone *preaching* to them?[5]

Without someone preaching the good news, the lost have less chance of hearing God's voice. Although salvation is available to everyone who calls on Christ, if they have not heard, how can they call on Him? Someone has to tell them, and no one will be told unless there is a preacher.

When God's servants preach under the anointing of the Holy Spirit, God is making Himself known and heard to us, and we must listen to what is being said. God has revealed preaching as His way of making Himself known. Titus 1:3 says that God "manifested His word through preaching."

John Stott writes, "It is God's speech that makes our speech necessary. We must speak what He has spoken. Hence the paramount obligation to preach." He goes on to state that this obligation is unique to Christianity. "Only Christian preachers claim to be heralds of good news from God, and dare to think of themselves as His ambassadors or representatives who actually utter oracles of God."[6]

Throughout the Bible, from the prophets to the apostles, preaching is given a central place. Godly messengers proclaimed God's message publicly by saying, "This is what God says." Through preaching, God reveals Himself. We can hear God by listening to what He has to say through godly preachers.

Godly counselors

I have found the best policy is to seek God and let Him choose how and through whom He wants to speak to us. If God chooses to speak to us through others, we should humbly receive from those God chooses to use. Proverbs tells us that our plans may fail if we refuse to take counsel from others, "Plans fail for lack of counsel, but with many advisers they succeed."[7]

The purpose of a "multitude of counselors" or "many advisors" is to receive a greater variety of wisdom. Obviously, we do not listen to just any person who gives us advice. The story is told of two destitute old men sitting on a park bench. One said, "I'm a man who never took advice from anybody."

The other man said, "Old buddy, I'm a man who followed everybody's advice!" When we are not selective about taking advice, it could lead to our ruin.

When listening to the godly counsel of others, it is some-times difficult to know if *you* have heard from God correctly or if *others* have heard accurately. The Bible urges us to "test the spirits."[8] If another believer claims to speak a word from God for you, test it. Ask God to confirm to you if it is really from Him.

If you have any doubts, go to your pastor or other proven Christian leader. These trusted leaders have traveled down the road before you, and they are examples of godly living. You can trust them for advice. Ask them to pray about it with you.

The Bible says that we should not just take counsel from anyone, but we should know the lives of those from whom we receive wisdom and direction, "...know those who labor among you—your leaders who are over you in the Lord and those who warn and kindly reprove and exhort you."[9]

Godly counselors are people who practice what they preach and have a track record of making good decisions. A godly counselor will be able to hear God's voice and confirm what God has been speaking to you. Godly counselors are those who love the Lord. You can trust them because they bear the good spiritual fruit of living close to Jesus.[10] Additionally, the benchmark of godly counselors is that they will be concerned about what happens after they give advice because they care about you and want to see you succeed.

If you came to me for advice, I would remind you that my responsibility is to help you to hear from God for yourself and to encourage you to be led by the Holy Spirit individually. If I know what the Word of God says about your particular situation, I will share it with you.

If I have a story from my life about how the Lord gave me direction in a similar situation, or if I have a particular discernment about your situation, I will share it. I cannot make the decision for you because it is not my responsibility to hear from God for you.

I learned this lesson the hard way. One time a Christian businessman came to me asking for advice regarding a business purchase that would cost him thousands of dollars. I told him to follow the peace of God in his heart and gave him some encouraging words. A year later, he told me he had lost money on this project and was not happy with my "advice." Rather than taking personal responsibility for his own decisions, I became the scapegoat for the failed deal. I am now much more cautious in giving advice to others without clarifying that they really must learn to hear from the Lord themselves. We should take the advice of others only when we also have our own peace about it after having prayed about it.

A godly counselor's goal is to give words of advice that confirm what you already feel in your own spirit, always leaving you to make the final decision on hearing God's voice.

You can hear God through people

Verse to remember

"...in a multitude of counselors there is safety" (Proverbs 24:6 NKJV).

Apply what you've learned

1. Why do you think there is "safety in a multitude of counselors?"
2. What is the danger of seeking others' opinions before God's?
3. How has a preacher or teacher helped you to hear God?
4. Have you ever experienced a time when you felt God speak something to you, and it was confirmed by another person? Describe how it helped you.

Chapter Eight

God speaks through
Common Sense Wisdom

O Lord, listen to my prayers; give me the common sense you promised (Psalm 119:169 LB)

The first time you go hiking and camping in the snow, you are told that certain things you do out in the wilderness are "simply common sense." You may not be sure what this means the *first* time you go winter camping, but you will soon realize that keeping your socks dry is "common sense." After one experience of wet socks and the consequences of frozen socks, the next time, your experience tells you that it is just common sense to keep your feet dry!

It is amazing to me that so many people seem to think that all their common sense must vanish in order for them to be really spiritual. It is often just the opposite. God gave us common sense as a gift from Him. I like to call it "common sense wisdom."

Common sense is an ability to look at things straightforwardly. This kind of common sense is mostly based on our experiences and not on our knowledge. In other words, our previous experiences add up to knowing intuitively what makes sense in a certain situation. As we

God trusts you, through the common sense He gives, to hear His voice.

accumulate more wisdom throughout life, we can automatically sense what to do in a certain situation because it is based on our past experiences. We can use our own sound judgment to make a decision.

Wisdom goes hand-in-hand with common sense. Straight thinking is the result of both experiences and wisdom. The Bible emphasizes that we should ask for wisdom. "If any of you lacks wisdom, he should ask God, who gives generously to all without finding fault, and it will be given to him."[1] Our God desires to give us wisdom if we only ask and believe; He will give it to us.

The book of Proverbs is a great source for common sense. I encourage you to read at least a few verses of Proverbs or Psalms regularly. The book of Psalms encourages us, builds us up and helps us express our innermost feelings. Proverbs, with its common sense wisdom, shows us how to stay out of trouble.

Slowly read through the following scriptures on common sense wisdom from the books of Psalms and Proverbs. These verses tell us it is possible for you and me to accumulate godly common sense wisdom.

> The man who knows right from wrong and has good judgment and common sense is happier than the man who is immensely rich! For such wisdom is far more valuable than precious jewels. Nothing else compares with it.[2]

> Have two goals: wisdom—that is, knowing and doing right—and common sense. Don't let them slip away, for they fill you with living energy and bring you honor and respect.[3]

> "Learn to be wise," he said, "and develop good judgment and common sense! I cannot overemphasize this point." [4]

Getting wisdom is the most important thing you can do! And with your wisdom, develop common sense and good judgment.[5]

Men with common sense are admired as counselors.[6]

A godly man gives good advice, but a rebel is destroyed by lack of common sense.[7]

A mocker never finds the wisdom he claims he is looking for, yet it comes easily to the man with common sense.[8]

Wisdom is enshrined in the hearts of men of common sense.[9]

The wise man is known by his common sense.[10]

... for I am your servant; therefore give me common sense to apply your rules to everything I do.[11]

If you want favor with both God and man, and a reputation for good judgment and common sense, then trust the Lord completely; don't ever trust yourself.[12]

A rebuke to a man of common sense is more effective than a hundred lashes on the back of a rebel.[13]

The man who strays away from common sense will end up dead![14]

Any enterprise is built by wise planning, becomes strong through common sense, and profits wonderfully by keeping abreast of the facts.[15]

If people would listen to the common sense wisdom that comes from God, they could spare themselves a lot of trouble. Common sense has a remarkable capacity to interpret our current situation in light of our history and God's Word. As we hear God speak to us, we can make a godly decision rather than a bad one.

Exercising common sense

Paul, the apostle, told the Corinthian Christians that they should learn to judge the small matters among themselves now, because at the end of this age, the resurrected saints will help to judge the world and even angels.[16] As Christians, we can learn to exercise good and wise judgment or common sense right now, in this life. Common sense allows us to make evaluations and assessments according to God's wisdom. God has given us a sound mind.

When we walk in the Spirit, we are in tune with God's voice, and can make common sense decisions according to God's will and wisdom. In Acts, the Jerusalem church leaders made a decision by saying, "It seemed good to the Holy Spirit and to us..." (15:28). God entrusts us as His children to use our common sense as we seek the Spirit's guidance.

Common sense will guide you when it comes to making monetary decisions. You will not go into debt when you do not spend more money than you earn. This fact is simple common sense wisdom. The Holy Spirit does not need to speak in an audible voice to tell us that we cannot have more money going out than we have coming in. This a no-brainer; it is common sense wisdom.

For the sake of example, let's say I am wondering if the Lord wants me to buy a new car. If I don't sense anything from God, then one of the common sense things I must ask myself is, "Can I afford it?" If I can't afford it, common sense wisdom is telling me not to buy it. The audible voice of God or a prophecy or a dream or a vision is not needed when common sense wisdom is already telling me what to do.

What if common sense clashes with peace?

Not everything that seems like common sense will be the voice of God speaking, however. Remember the story earlier about the man who was offered a fantastic job with a large company where he would make a huge salary? Common sense would lead him to believe that the job offered everything he needed to provide financially for his family. Nevertheless, he did not have peace about taking the job and knew that in this situation, he could not make a decision based on common sense when his heart was unsettled.

I grew up as an only son. My father trained me to operate the family farm with the eventual goal to own it. When the Lord began to call me in the late 1970's toward being a full-time pastor, I just did not have God's peace about staying on the farm. Although it seemed like common sense to stay in a career that I had been trained in, it clashed with my peace of mind. I knew the Lord was speaking to me about giving up the opportunity to own the farm and instead giving myself to serving as a pastor of a local church for the next 15 years.

What if God's voice seems the opposite of common sense?

There are times when God speaks and it will go against what you think is common sense. I am sure the widow in 1 Kings 17 had second thoughts about giving her last flour and oil to Elijah. It just did not make sense to make a meal for Elijah when she and her son were about to starve. But Elijah told the widow that God had spoken, and the flour and oil would not run dry. Their obedience to the Lord's voice caused a supernatural miracle of abundance.

God's voice seemed the opposite of common sense in another biblical story in 2 Kings 5. The prophet Elisha told Naaman to dip himself in the Jordan river seven times and he would be healed of leprosy. Common sense might tell you that washing yourself in a dirty river would not be good for your health. Additionally, common sense would tell you that if you dipped in one time and were not cured, six more times wouldn't do it either. But Naaman chose to trust that God was speaking through the prophet even though it did not make sense. He kept dipping himself seven times until he was healed.

God trusts you with common sense

When we do not get a "rhema" message from God, we need to use common sense wisdom in the choices we make. A friend of mine was seeking God's voice as to which local congregation he was to attend. As he prayed, he sensed the Lord saying, "You decide; the choice is yours; I've given you the ability to know which church is best for you and your family."

I have found that if God doesn't speak to me specifically, it does not mean He is not leading me. There are some issues about which God already trusts me and you to know what is right or wrong and the way we should go. We don't need a "specific word" from God; however, we must always stay open to waiting on Him to see if there is a need for Him to intervene in the way we are planning to go or in the choices we are making.

God tells us to do the seeking, and He does the speaking. We can be assured that He is the Spirit of wisdom and He will not lead us to do things or make decisions that are unwise.

You can hear God through common sense wisdom

Verse to remember "The wise man is known by his common sense" (Proverbs 16:21 LB).

Apply what you've learned:
1. How do wisdom and common sense go hand-in-hand?
2. Have you ever been in a situation when something that seemed like common sense was not God speaking? What did you do?
3. Did God's voice ever seem the opposite of common sense? What did you do?
4. Describe a time you experienced God speaking to you through common sense wisdom.

Chapter Nine

God speaks through
Conviction

Conviction moves us to hunger for more of God.

God speaks to us by giving us an ever-deepening conviction and awareness of His presence in our daily lives. He not only wants us to listen so He can tell us what to do, but He also wants us to listen so we know what *not* to do. This is His conviction.

Jesus said He would send the Holy Spirit to indwell us and convict us of sin.[1] When the Holy Spirit convicts us, we see just how desperately we need God. God doesn't convict us of our sins to expose us and make us feel bad. Instead, He wants to make us feel desperate for Him, realizing we have no confidence in ourselves.

Oswald Chambers once said,

> Conviction of sin is one of the most uncommon things that ever happens to a person. It is the beginning of an understanding of God. Jesus Christ said that when the Holy Spirit came He would convict people of sin. And when the Holy Spirit stirs a person's conscience and brings him into the presence of God, it is not that person's relationship with others that bothers him but his relationship with God.[2]

God's voice of conviction draws you closer to God.

Conviction moves us to look at what God offers and challenges us to know this infinite, loving and almighty heavenly Father.

The Holy Spirit speaks to our conscience to convict us of any sin and gives us a disposition toward righteousness. The Holy Spirit's conviction is intended to convince us to repent, which means to turn and go in the right direction rather than the wrong one.

In other words, if we are behaving in a way that is not pleasing to God, we must be willing to make an adjustment in our lives. If we don't, our hearts become hardened. Hardened hearts are the result of ignoring the Holy Spirit's conviction of right and wrong. The more hard-hearted we become, the more difficult it is for us to quickly hear and promptly obey the Lord.

If I am angry at someone, bitterness can grow in my heart. If, however, I allow the Holy Spirit and the Word of God to quickly prompt me to forgive, I can receive grace to move on and hear the Lord speak accurately. I can depend on God to convict me to do what is right.

God's adjustment

God loves to transform people. It is a promise in His Word. He said that He would take our unnaturally hardened hearts out and instead give us a heart of flesh, a heart that is sensitive to the touch of our God.[3]

My friend Dave recalls how God sought to make an adjustment in his life by convicting him of his self-righteousness. During his college years, he was becoming increasingly cynical of religious people who seemed to be playing church. He was repulsed by the smug insincerity that he saw. Then one day God's voice spoke in quiet but forceful conviction, "So, how about you? Are you sincere? Are you taking Me seriously?" Dave saw his self-righteous sin and repented. His attitude changed from that day onward.

Some time after I received Jesus Christ as my Lord, the Holy Spirit convicted me of cheating when I remembered I had deceived a classmate in high school. Another friend and I were gambling with him and had rigged it so that he always lost. I wrote to the classmate, explained what had happened and asked him for forgiveness, returning the money that I had taken from him, with interest. God convicted me so that I could make an adjustment in my life and hear from God with a clear conscience.

Conviction vs. condemnation

True conviction is entirely different from condemnation. God's voice will bring conviction over sin and a way out. The enemy's voice will bring condemnation and no way out. For example, Satan may say to you, "You know, you never pray enough" or "If you would read your Bible more, God would love you more." Condemnation is shame-based and accuses us in our character.

Conviction arouses hope. It moves us beyond failure and causes us to want to know God more fully and deeply. It is about a specific sin, rather than a general accusation of character.

The devil condemns us, but God convicts us. Condemnation brings doubt, fear, unbelief and hopelessness. God convicts us to restore us to righteousness and faith. He always corrects us to build us up, and His conviction always brings hope and a way of escape.

> No temptation has seized you except what is common to man. And God is faithful; he will not let you be tempted beyond what you can bear. But when you are tempted, he will also provide a way out so that you can stand up under it.[4]

It is so important to discern the truth and know the difference between conviction and condemnation. If you respond to the Lord's conviction, you will be lifted up and out of sin; however, condemnation only makes you feel bad about yourself. It is healthy and normal to feel guilty when we are initially convicted of sin; however, if we keep feeling guilty after we have repented, it is spiritually unhealthy.

We could sum it up this way—conviction is our friend. It is God speaking to us about His limits, providing protection for us. Satan's goal through condemnation is to bring us into bondage— bondage to shame and false guilt.

The finger of conviction

It is good to know that the Holy Spirit doesn't spring everything on us at once. He usually convicts us to change or make adjustments in our lives when He knows we are ready. If it is not the right time to face something, then the Lord usually will not convict us of it.

The Lord invites us to approach Him without fear. The Bible says He wants to help us in our time of need. "Let us then approach the throne of grace with confidence, so that we may receive mercy and find grace to help us in our time of need."[5] If we have sin in our lives, our heavenly Father still loves us. He wants us to come boldly to His throne and receive His forgiveness, His grace and His mercy!

God clearly spoke to Liz about working with teens by placing His finger of conviction on her life. One evening, Liz was sitting in her small group meeting and started to squirm. She felt God's finger of conviction on her life, but didn't immediately know why. Was there sin in her life? The feeling of conviction was strong. She felt as though there was a fire under her chair!

A few days later, one of the fathers of the teens in her small group called. He asked if she would be willing to work with another adult to lead a small group especially for teens. She stepped out into youth ministry at that time, realizing that if God had not convicted her a few days before the request, she probably would have said "no."

God's conviction fell on a bakery owner in Bristol, England, while George Mueller was praying for food for his orphanages which relied solely on contributions to feed the children. The children were in dire need of food, and George was praying for this need. God awakened a bakery owner across town who felt God's conviction to get up, call an employee, and ask him to go to the shop to bake a day's bread for the orphans. Then on second thought, he told the employee, "Bake enough for a month so I can get some sleep."

God is speaking to us when He convicts us. This conviction might come from an inner prompting of God's still, small voice, reading the Word of God or from hearing a sermon preached or in some other way. God convicts us so we can be released to move forward in His grace and mercy as we continue to develop a sensitivity to hear His voice.

You can hear God through conviction

Verse to remember "When he comes, he will convict the world of guilt in regard to sin and righteousness and judgment" (John 16:8).

Apply what you've learned
1. How does conviction stir your conscience to want to know God better?
2. Have you ever ignored the Holy Spirit's conviction and your heart became hardened?
3. Can you distinguish between condemnation and conviction of the Holy Spirit? If not, what can you do to make this distinction?
4. Describe a time the Lord spoke to you through conviction.

Chapter Ten

God speaks through
Worship

You exist to bring pleasure to God through worship.

You were made for God's fellowship, and your heart will
never be satisfied without it. God wants you to love Him deeply
and bring pleasure to Him through your worship and devotion.
The Bible says, "The Lord is pleased only with those who worship him and trust his love."[1]

Jesus responds to your worship. One day a sinful woman
came to Jesus, weeping. Her heart was deeply stirred with her
love for Jesus, and she stood crying beside Him with her tears
wetting His feet. She then knelt down and kissed His feet as she
poured an expensive perfume on them, revealing her lavish love
for her Lord. This woman had tried to fulfill her longing for love
from men, but now she had found the Lover of her soul. She was
not ashamed to express that love openly and freely. She knew she
could trust the Lord.

Indeed, upon receiving her
act of worship, Jesus spoke to
her. He responded to her
worship by telling her that her
sins were forgiven and she
should go in peace.[2]

**Worship places you
in a position to hear
from God.**

Worship is a lifelong conversation and love affair between
you and God as you surrender your life to Him. Worship is often

Hearing God

mistakenly relegated to our participation in a church service, when we "praise and worship the Lord." Of course, when we surrender our hearts to the Lord and worship Him with music and singing in a church service, we will hear God's voice, but worship involves so much more.

Worship is a life-style of bringing pleasure to God by the way you live your life. Rick Warren wrote, "Every activity can be transformed into an act of worship when you do it for the praise, glory, and pleasure of God."[3] The Bible says, "So whether you eat or drink or whatever you do, do it all for the glory of God."[4]

Martin Luther observed, "A dairymaid can milk cows to the glory of God."

Olympic runner Eric Liddel maintained, "When I run, I feel His pleasure." Running was an act of worship for him.

There really are no formulas for worship because worship is a function of the heart. If you do everything as if you are doing it for Jesus, even everyday chores are an act of worship.

Jesus said that all worship must take place "in spirit and in truth."[5] You communicate with God through your spirit. Your spirit intuitively senses God's presence and receives revelation from Him.

Sometimes the lyrics of a song suddenly become personal, giving insight or direction in a timely way. You may be listening to a worship music CD, participating in a worship service or mowing your lawn, and the Lord speaks clearly to you. Because you are focusing on Him and giving Him your undivided attention and love, you are in a position to hear clearly what the Lord is speaking to you.

He inhabits our praise

God says He inhabits the praises of His people.[6] When you live a life of praise to your God, God is in your midst. The devil, who dwells in darkness, hates it when we praise and worship God because it reminds him of his past when he was overseeing the choirs of heaven.

Amy Carmichael said, "I believe truly that Satan cannot endure it and so slips out of the room—more or less!—When there is a true song. Prayer rises more easily, more spontaneously, after one has let those wings, words, and music, carry one out of oneself into that upper air."[7]

When we are "carried into that upper air," joyfully basking in the presence of God, we will hear God speak. I often receive messages from the Lord while I am worshiping in His presence. When the Lord called me to start a new church when I was in my twenties, it was during a worship service in my local church in Pennsylvania.

If you are worshiping the Lord and He speaks something to you, write down what He says. It might be for today, next week, next month, or a year from now or a decade from now. Write it down so you do not forget what the Lord has spoken. Later, often many years later, you will be wonderfully surprised at what you had written.

Learning to be thankful

Thankfulness is an act of worship. God's general will for you is to "give thanks in all circumstances; for this is the will of God in Christ Jesus for you."[8] When you have learned to obey His will right where you are by being thankful, you don't have to worry about what God will speak to you. You will be ready today to hear His voice in the future.

Thankfulness keeps your ears and mind open to hearing God speak to you. The Bible says you are to thank God *in* everything, not *for* everything. That means that no matter what is going on in your life, you are not to complain, murmur, grumble, or find fault. God doesn't want to hear you grumbling because grumbling is evidence that you have no faith in His ability to make things better.

After telling us to thank God in everything, the very next verse says, "Do not quench the Spirit."[9] We can quench the Holy Spirit through complaining. Grumblers have a very hard time

Hearing God

hearing from God. The Bible says: "Do everything without complaining or arguing."[10] It's our natural tendency to complain. Anyone can do it. But it is supernatural to give thanks amidst life's tests and trials.

Worship has the ability to help us get our eyes off of our problems or situation and onto the Lord Jesus. It is self-correcting, like a clock that resets itself to the right time every 24 hours. We should choose to worship every day. Giving thanks is the will of God for all of us. Unthankful people quickly enter into deception and find it very hard to hear the clear, pure Word of the Lord.

Jesus said, "If you live in Me and My words remain in you and continue to live in your hearts, ask whatever you will, and it shall be done for you."[11] God wants our hearts. Jesus did not fail to respond to the woman who anointed His feet with perfume as her act of worship and adoration. And He will respond to you too. He is eager to speak to you. Just love Him!

You can hear God through worship

Verse to remember

"Give thanks in all circumstances, for this is God's will for you in Christ Jesus" (1 Thessalonians 5:18).

Apply what you've learned
1. Tell how you can make worship a life-style.
2. How can God "inhabit our praise?"
3. Explain how thankfulness keeps our ears and minds open to hearing from God.
4. Tell of a time you know God spoke to you through worship.

Chapter Eleven

God speaks through
Authorities

Honoring and respecting authority releases you to hear from God.

A contemporary Christian musician wanted to record her music; however, her parents asked her to wait. She found it difficult, but made a decision to submit to her parents. She later produced a recording that has been a blessing to hundreds of thousands of people. God blessed this musician and gave her the right timing for the release of her recording by honoring and submitting to her parents.

Since mankind's fall had its source in rebellion, and rebellion disrupts authority, we will have trouble hearing God's voice if we rebel against the authorities God has set in place for us. If we respect and honor these authorities, we open the channel for communication with God. Authorities help us with the

Honoring authorities in your life opens a channel for communication with God.

timing of the Lord's direction, and God uses them to help build character in our lives.

All authority comes from God. Since the beginning of time, God has ruled and upheld the universe with His authority. God delegated authority to his Son: "All authority has been given to

Me in heaven and on earth,"[1] and under the authority of Jesus are levels of earthly authority.

God carries out His authority through four God-ordained human institutions: government, parents, employers and church leaders. When we honor and respect teachers, employers, police officers, our church leadership and our parents, we are honoring Christ.

Submitting to the authorities actually protects us. For example, if we disobey the speed limit, we could be killed or kill someone else. If a parent tells a child not to play with matches and he disobeys, there could be the loss of a home or the loss of life. It would not be the parents' fault or God's fault; the child simply disobeyed the authority that was placed in his life. He moved out from under the umbrella of God's protection.

We'll have trouble hearing God if we rebel

Peter urged the Christian believers to "be subject for the Lord's sake to every human institution...."[2] If we rebel against any of these established human institutions, we violate God's divine authority. We are going to have trouble hearing God's voice if rebellion and disrespect cloud our lives.

This is not to say that we cannot question authority in our lives. We should raise some questions: "Is this a legitimate use of authority?" "Should this really be done this way?" If the questions are asked in a spirit of humility and respect, it is not wrong to ask them.

The Bible says that the powers that be are ordained of God, "Everyone must submit himself to the governing authorities, for there is no authority except that which God has established. The authorities that exist have been established by God. Consequently, he who rebels against the authority is rebelling against what God has instituted, and those who do so will bring judgment on themselves."[3]

This scripture does not mean that God endorses everything that civil governments do, but since God brings government to pass, we should submit to those in charge out of respect for God. Although this scripture is talking about submitting to governing authorities, it applies to all authorities in our lives. If I am careless in obeying earthly authority, I place myself in a position of disobedience to the ultimate authority that stands behind the earthly—God's authority. We apply this when we remind our children that if they do not learn to respect their parents they will have trouble respecting anyone or anything else.

Hearing God through authorities protects us

Having an attitude of submission toward the authorities God has placed in our lives will protect us from many mistakes. I was talking to a new believer who was lamenting about a parole officer giving him input he did not like. I explained to him that God probably was speaking through that parole officer and using her words to speak into his life.

An attitude of submission is also a protection against the influence of the devil. The nature of the devil is rebellion and deceit. Lucifer fell from heaven because he said, "I will be like the Most High."[4] He refused to submit to God's authority. Whenever we allow an attitude of rebellion into our lives, we are beginning to be motivated by the enemy, which leads us to sin against God.

Hearing God through authorities trains us in character

Yet another blessing we receive from learning to submit to the authorities in our lives is that it trains us in character.

The Lord uses leadership in the church to speak the Word of God to us. His Word chips away from our lives anything that is not from Him. Just as a blacksmith takes a piece of iron, makes it hot so that it becomes pliable and chips the impurities away with his hammer, God's Word purifies. "'Is not my word like fire,' declares the Lord...."[5] It destroys all that is false in our lives and leaves only the genuine metal. In the same way, our character is strengthened as we become conformed into the image of Christ.

Hearing God

God placed authorities in our lives to make us pliable. When we react to authority in anger and bitterness because we do not get our own way, it is probably a sign that there are still impurities the Lord wants to chip away from our lives. The Word of God is a purifying fire that changes us more into His likeness.

Hearing God through authorities provides guidance

Submitting to the authority the Lord has placed in our lives often provides guidance for us to know His will. As a young man, my parents asked me to break off my relationship with certain ungodly friends. At the time, I did not appreciate what they were telling me. I felt controlled; but in retrospect, I am thankful to God for giving me the grace to submit to their authority. I realize now, it saved me from having my life shipwrecked. God spoke to me through the authority of my parents.

Joseph, in the Old Testament, submitted to the authority of the jailer, even though he was falsely imprisoned. The Lord later raised him up as prime minister for the nation.

Jesus Himself submitted to His heavenly Father every day. Jesus said, "...for I seek not to please myself but him who sent me."[6] Jesus was committed to walking in submission to His heavenly Father's authority. Jesus did nothing of his own initiative, but only that which was initiated by His heavenly Father. He also spent the early years of His life submitting to His earthly father in the carpentry shop.

Appeal to authority if they are wrong

This brings us to a very important question. "What should I do if the authority in my life is wrong?" The Bible makes it clear that if any person in authority in our lives requires us to sin, we must obey God and not man.[7] If the authorities in our lives are asking us to cheat, steal, lie or sin in any way, we must obey the living God first! The early church leaders were told by the religious leaders of their day to stop proclaiming Jesus as Lord. They could not obey these orders; however, they still maintained a spirit and attitude of honoring the religious leaders.

What if we believe the godly authority in our lives is not sinning, but making a mistake? Philippians 4:6 tells us to make an appeal. "Do not be anxious about anything, but in everything, by prayer and petition, with thanksgiving, present your requests to God."

First of all, we need to appeal to God. We should pray, making known our requests and concerns, as we appeal to Him as our authority. In the same way, this sets a precedent for us to appeal to the delegated authorities in our lives.

A friend of mine was required to sign a job-related document but realized that the technical wording would make him sign an untruth. He prayed and decided that he needed to obey God. Before he went to his supervisors to appeal to them, he asked the Lord for wisdom to fulfill his employer's intentions without compromising the truth. The Lord showed him a plan, but he was prepared to give up his job if required.

He told his supervisors he appreciated working at the company and explained why he could not sign the document. He admitted that it might inconvenience them or that he could lose his job; still, he needed to be faithful to God and not tell a lie. On his own time, he volunteered to make the change on the format of the document so it legally fulfilled their company's purpose at the same time.

They accepted his idea, and the Lord gave him tremendous favor in that company. Appealing to authorities with an attitude of submission will open the doors for us to hear God speak.

Instead of having a submissive spirit and appealing to authority, Aaron and Miriam accused Moses regarding the leadership decisions that He was making. They did not fear God or respect God's prophet, and this allowed a spirit of rebellion to come into their lives. Moses, who had learned his lesson about authority in the desert while herding sheep, did not defend himself. Instead he went to God, and God defended him.

Daniel and his friends, in the Old Testament, appealed to the authority in their lives and asked only to eat certain foods.[8] The Lord honored their appeal to authority and blessed them with health, wisdom, literary skill and supernatural revelation.

Nehemiah appealed to the king to take a trip to Jerusalem.[9] His appeal to the authority in his life in an attitude of submission caused the king to grant his request. Nehemiah's attitude and obedience made it possible for the wall to be built around Jerusalem.

An attitude of love and submission toward those God has placed in authority in our lives releases us to hear Him speak. This is often quite the opposite of what our selfish nature wants—to be right in our own eyes and "do our own thing."

God's intention is to use the authorities He has placed in our lives to help mold and structure our lives for good. In many cases, the Lord is actually speaking to us through these individuals. Listening to these authorities opens the door for us to hear His voice.

You can hear God through authorities

Verse to remember "Everyone must submit himself to the governing authorities, for there is no authority except that which God has established. The authorities that exist have been established by God" (Romans 13:1).

Apply what you've learned
1. What often happens when we rebel against authority?
2. How does submitting to authority train us in character?
3. Have you ever appealed to your pastor, parent, employer or the government because they were wrong? Give examples.
4. Tell how honoring and respecting authority has released you to hear from God.

Hearing God

Chapter Twelve

God speaks through
Natural Things

Creation shouts out God's glory continuously, completely and clearly.

I love to go to the ocean. I experience the Lord's majestic power at the sea shore. The ocean is so amazingly massive, and yet the mighty roaring waves stop at a certain place because God has commanded them to go no farther. Sitting by the ocean, I gain great strength as I watch the pounding waves. They speak to me of the vast strength and awesomeness of the Lord. I also love the mountains where I experience God's majesty in the breathtaking views across a valley or the snow-capped peaks in the distance. God speaks to me through the nature that He has created.

The Bible confirms that God reveals Himself through nature. "The heavens declare the glory of God; the skies proclaim the work of his hands...."[1] Psalm 29 says,

> The voice of the Lord is over the waters; the God of
> glory thunders...The voice of the Lord is powerful;
> the voice of the Lord is majestic. The voice of the
> Lord breaks the cedars...the voice of the Lord strikes
> with flashes of lightening. The voice of the Lord
> shakes the desert...The voice of the Lord twists the

God constantly reveals Himself to you through nature.

oaks and strips the forest bare. And in his temple, all cry, "Glory!"

In nature, we discover a nonstop manifestation of God. Nature sends a clear signal that everyone can receive.

God told Abraham to look at the stars to get a vision of his future family. The vast starry sky symbolized the countless ancestors that God promised He would give Abraham.[2]

From the beginning of creation, God has shown what His eternal power and character are like by all He has made.[3] Even those who are not living in the will of God can perceive right from wrong and instinctively know that God exists because nature itself testifies of His existence. That's why people cannot claim ignorance of God as an excuse for refusing to honor Him. Atheists will some day stand before the Lord and realize that God spoke through His handiwork and they ignored this revelation in nature.[4]

It was through the very intricate design of God's handiwork—a child—that God spoke to the American writer, Whittaker Chambers, when he was still an atheist. He was observing his infant daughter and was struck by the fact that such an exquisite creature was not an accident or a freak of nature. He recalls in his autobiography:

> I was sitting in our apartment...my daughter was in her high chair. I was watching her eat. She was the most miraculous thing that had ever happened in my life...My eye came to rest on the delicate convolutions of her ear—those intricate, perfect ears. The thought passed through my mind: "No, those ears were not created by any chance coming together of atoms in nature. They could have been created only by immense design." The thought was involuntary and unwanted. I crowded it out of my mind.... I did not then know that, at that moment, the finger of God was first laid upon my forehead.[5]

God revealed Himself clearly in the design of a child. Mr Chambers could not ignore God's voice speaking to him.

While on this earth, Jesus often used natural things to teach spiritual lessons so we could more clearly understand how God communicates with mankind. Jesus told us to consider the lilies of the field[6] and the ravens of the air.[7] Meditating on how God adorns the fields and provides for the birds will remind us that if He cares so completely for nature, He cares even more deeply for mankind whom He made in His own image.

In the parable of the farmer and the seed, Jesus used a natural phenomenon like a seed sprouting and growing to teach us the spiritual truth that when the message of the gospel is sown in our hearts, it produces growth and fruitfulness spontaneously.[8]

The Pharisees pretended they wanted to see evidence that Jesus was the Messiah by asking Him to show them a great demonstration in the skies.[9] Although Jesus could have caused lightening to strike at their feet or thunder to roll, He chose not to show a natural sign to speak to them because their hearts were wicked and obstinate. They would not have believed anyway.

Another time, Jesus told a parable of a budding fig tree, giving proof that summer is near, to speak symbolically of the proof that one day Israel would return to the Promised Land and form a sovereign state once again.[10] Again, God was speaking to mankind through a natural sign to make it easier to understand.

Many times God revealed His presence in the form of a cloud. A cloud led God's people out of Egypt as a cloud by day and a pillar of fire by night.[11] A cloud settled down on the tabernacle, filling it with God's glory.[12] The same thing happened when Solomon finished building the temple.[13] The cloud symbolized the glory of God's majesty and presence that filled the temple. God was speaking His blessing as He took up residence in the temple.

Through the observation of life situations and natural phenomena, the Lord often speaks a lesson or insight. Learning to observe and listen for God to speak through nature is a very fruitful way to learn from God.

God reveals Himself through nature

Every morning the sun comes up, and every evening it goes down. The stars come out in the sky, and the universe remains in order as a reminder that God is watching over us each day. He keeps the planets in place, broadcasting His unfathomable power and glory as the solar system travels along God's predetermined orbit.

If He can hold the sun and the stars in place, we can be assured that He is able to keep our lives in order too. While traveling in northern Scotland I experienced the pristine stars of Scotland. (Since Scotland suffers less than other developed countries from urban glare light distractions, the stars are quite magnificent.) I felt so close to the Lord as I again experienced God's enormity and love. The Lord comforted and encouraged me through His natural creation. I knew without a doubt that God held the world in His hand and no matter what was wrong in the world, He would sustain me because He is the Creator.

Where I live in Pennsylvania, the deciduous trees stretch their bare limbs to the sky, revealing a stark, surreal look in the wintertime. Yet, these same trees come back to life each spring as their leaves bud once again and they fill out with fresh, beautiful foliage. It reminds us that God will bring our lives back into full bloom even if we feel our present circumstances are dismal.

Along with the many other ways God speaks, look for God to speak through His creation to send a clear signal to you that He cares.

You can hear God through natural things

Verse to remember "The heavens declare the glory of God; the skies proclaim the work of his hands" (Psalm 19:1).

Apply what you've learned

1. How does God show His character through what He has made in nature?
2. How can people perceive right from wrong through nature?
3. Tell of a time Jesus taught a lesson through nature.
4. How has God revealed Himself to you through nature?

Chapter Thirteen

God speaks through
The Church

God's assignments are usually too big for you to accomplish on your own. With this in mind, He provides other believers with whom you can have regular fellowship who can also help you hear from God. Although we live in a large global planet that links us with someone halfway across the world with the click of an internet connection, communication alone does not give us the authentic fellowship we need with other people. What people are looking for today are real relationships that offer a genuine connection with others that gives them a real sense of being understood and loved. Within this busy world, where can we find this kind of *bona fide* fellowship with others? We can find it in the church— the body of Christ where a community of believers interact to encourage each other to hear from God.

I once read the story of a young man who had given his life to God; but

God uses those in the church as His mouthpiece to speak to you.

after a time of disappointment and disillusionment, he began to withdraw from other Christians. The young man's pastor stopped in for a visit one cold, blustery winter evening and with the wind howling outside, they sat and talked.

After awhile, the wise pastor walked over to the fireplace, and with a pair of prongs picked up a hot coal from the fire, placing it on the bricks in front of the fireplace. He continued to converse with the young man. Then glancing at the ember on the bricks, he said, "Do you see that piece of coal? While it was in the fireplace it burned brightly, but now that it's alone, the ember has almost gone out."

The pastor walked over to the fireplace, and with the prongs, picked up the ember and placed it inside the fireplace. Within minutes, the dying ember was again burning brightly.

It suddenly dawned on the young man what the pastor was trying to tell him. When we move away from the warmth and encouraging fires of fellow believers in the body of Christ, we will eventually cool down spiritually. Joining with others as a community of believers in a local church body helps keep our fires glowing. From that day on, the young man made a decision to join regularly with other believers in a local church in his community. He did not want to take the chance of his fire going out again.

Hearing God through the support system of a spiritual family

The Bible says, "But encourage one another daily, as long as it is called Today, so that none of you may be hardened by sin's deceitfulness."[1] It is extremely difficult to live the Christian life alone. Believers need to fellowship together and encourage one another daily.

The church is not a building or a meeting or a program. The church of Jesus Christ is simply *people*. As believers, we are the church. The word *church* literally means *called out ones*. The church then, is a group of people who have been called out of spiritual darkness into the light of God's kingdom.

When we come to Christ, we are immediately a part of the universal church of Christ which includes every believer who has ever named the name of Christ from every nation of the world. Jesus talks about His universal church in the gospels. "And I tell you that you are Peter, and on this rock I will build my church, and the gates of Hades will not overcome it."[2]

I have had the privilege of traveling to six continents of the world. Everywhere I go, I find believers from completely different backgrounds, different skin colors and cultures who have one thing in common. They all have received Jesus Christ as Lord and are part of the same family. They are the body of Christ worldwide. Paul, the apostle, recognized this global church when he said, "For this reason I kneel before the Father, from whom his whole family in heaven and on earth derives its name."[3]

But the word *church* also refers to the *local* church—the local body of Christ. Within God's universal church family are *local* churches in each community which provide the support and love each believer needs. Whether you are a part of a local community church, a large mega church or a small house church, the Lord wants to speak to you through the leadership there and through fellow believers.

Every believer needs a "support system" to survive. We get that support system from being committed to other believers in a local church and having regular fellowship with them. We are a part of a spiritual family—a family of the redeemed. This spiritual family gives us a place to grow and learn from other believers how to live our Christian lives. We need this input from others.

Sometimes, through disillusionment, disappointment or spiritual pride, believers find themselves uninvolved in a local church. This leaves them very vulnerable. The Bible tells us that "No temptation has seized you except what is common to man. And God is faithful; he will not let you be tempted beyond what you can bear. But when you are tempted, he will also provide a way out so that you can stand up under it."[4]

The local church is often "the way out" the Lord has prepared for His people during an onslaught of the devil. When we fellowship with other believers, we realize that we are not alone in the temptations that we face. We receive spiritual protection, strength and oversight from the spiritual leaders the Lord has placed in our lives. The Lord's plan is to use the local church to protect us, help us grow, and equip us to be all that we can be in Jesus Christ.

D.L. Moody, an evangelist from the late 1800's, was used of the Lord to lead a million people to Christ. Many times when he preached, he had a choir that included singers from many churches in the community in which he was preaching. A lady came to him one day and said, "Mr. Moody, I would like to sing in your choir." When Moody asked her which local church she represented, she said, "I am involved in the universal church."

Moody said to her, "Then find the pastor of the universal church and sing in his choir." In other words, Moody was concerned about this lady's lack of involvement in a local church. He recognized the need to be committed to a local church for spiritual protection and accountability. Though the church is not perfect, God designed the church to be a blessing to believers. The church might have a few spots and wrinkles, but she is still engaged to the bridegroom and He is committed to make her beautiful.

Church leaders and other believers act as God's mouthpiece

Spiritual leaders as well as other believers in the local church are there to exhort you, comfort you and uphold you in prayer. God places spiritual leaders in our lives who are accountable to God and to other spiritual leaders to watch out for us.

> Remember your leaders, who spoke the word of God to you. Consider the outcome of their way of life and imitate their faith. Obey your leaders and submit to their authority. They keep watch over you as men who must give an account. Obey them so that their work will be a joy, not a burden, for that would be of no advantage to you.[5]

Spiritual leaders in our lives give us spiritual protection, and we need to follow their example as they place their faith in Jesus Christ. We should remember them, receive the Word of God from them, obey them, be submissive to them, and do all that we can so their responsibility is joyful and not a burden. God often uses them as His mouthpiece to speak to us. The Bible tells us that the devil is like a roaring lion seeking to devour us.[6] Lions prey on strays, those who are isolated from the herd. That's why we need church leaders—to protect us and encourage us. The Lord has called us to recognize and honor those He has placed in our lives as spiritual leaders.

> Now we ask you, brothers, to respect those who work hard among you, who are over you in the Lord and who admonish you. Hold them in the highest regard in love because of their work. Live in peace with each other. [7]

I have spent much of my time traveling to various nations of the world in the past years, and I have been blessed over and over again by the spiritual leaders that the Lord has placed in my life. Our small group leaders, local pastors and elders have provided a tremendous sense of encouragement and protection to me and my family.

Many times these precious brothers and sisters in Christ have prayed, encouraged and exhorted us. The Lord has used these spiritual leaders who have encouraged me and held me accountable to take enough time with my family even though my travel schedule can be demanding. I am grateful to the Lord for using spiritual leaders in my life to speak to me again and again over the past years because I know I cannot do it on my own.

Because you cannot accomplish all you want on your own, God will be faithful to speak to you through the spiritual leaders and fellow believers He has placed in your life.

You can hear God through the church

Verse to remember "Obey your leaders and submit to their authority. They keep watch over you as men who must give an account. Obey them so that their work will be a joy, not a burden, for that would be of no advantage to you" (Hebrews 13:17).

Apply what you've learned

1. Why is a community of believers so important to hearing from God?
2. Explain how you receive a support system from the local church.
3. How has God used those in the church as His mouthpiece to speak to you?

Chapter Fourteen

God speaks through
His Character

God is love and He responds to us by His loving character.

After more than 30 years of a loving marriage, I know the character of my wife LaVerne. I am confident that she would not intentionally speak harmful words or make rash decisions that would hurt me or betray me. All of her actions, including words of correction, are for my own good because she loves me. I trust her. I trust her character.

How we see the character of God affects our relationship with Him. Since God will never tell us to do anything that is outside His character, we must get to know the very nature of God so we can be sure we are hearing from Him. We must understand His compassionate nature and how He longs for our intimacy and trust.

One of the most familiar verses in the Bible states, "For God so loved the world...."[1] God's nature is revealed in this revelation of God as the Lover of mankind. God is love[2] and He loves us. We are precious in His sight and He yearns for us. He wants to reveal Himself to us. He is passionately pursuing us!

You know you are hearing God's voice when it matches the character and words of Jesus.

The familiar scripture verse goes on to say that God so loved the world that "He gave...." He not only wants us to be lovers of people as He is, He wants us to be givers. He wants us to act like He does—to live by His character. For example, He always tells the truth. He sets the example for us to do the same and be truthful people, true to our word.

The Bible tells us that God "...made known His ways to Moses, His acts to the children of Israel." [3] Because Moses was in relationship with the Lord, he had learned to know the character of the Lord; however, the children of Israel only saw the things that God did because they did not have a personal relationship with Him. When we get to know God and develop a love relationship with Him, we will know what God wants us to do. He will "make known" His ways to us.

God reveals Himself through His love

1 Corinthians 13:4-8 offers us a description of what love is. When we substitute "God" for "love" in these verses, we get an accurate picture of God's character. "God is patient, God is kind, God does not envy, God does not boast, God is not proud, God is not rude, God is not self-seeking, God is not easily angered, God keeps no record of wrongs, God does not delight in evil but rejoices with the truth, God always protects, God always trusts, God always hopes, God always perseveres, God never fails."

God's love is revealed so that mankind can be liberated. The scriptures tell us the Lord is one "who forgives all your iniquities, who heals all your diseases, who redeems your life from destruction, who crowns you with lovingkindness and tender mercies."[4] This is who our God is! He is a God who is forgiving and a God of healing who wants to redeem our lives from destruction. What does it mean for God to redeem us?

The word *redeemed* means *to buy back*. I've heard the story of a young boy, who after spending many hours constructing a little boat, took it out on the lake to sail it. With a long string attached to the boat, the boy was having a great time as the boat floated and bobbed. Suddenly, the string tore. In an instant, he lost his prized possession and could only watch as the boat headed downstream where it eventually exited into the river. He thought it was gone forever.

Several years later, this lad entered a pawn shop in a town downstream from where he grew up. He spotted the boat that he had built years before. The young man approached the store-keeper and said, "This is my boat. My initials are carved on the bottom."

The owner said, "Well, I'm sorry, but somebody brought that boat into my store and I bought it from him. You'll need to pay me for it." The young man immediately paid the shopkeeper so he could buy back his cherished boat.

This is a picture of what God did for us. God made you and me. As we went our own way, He loved us so much He redeemed us and bought us back again at great cost—the cost of His Son's life.

We hear God through Jesus

When you responded to God's offer of reconciliation that is possible because of Jesus' death on a cross, a marvelous transfor-mation occurred. You become a brand new person. You are a new creation in Jesus Christ. The Bible says in 2 Corinthians 5:17, "Therefore, if anyone is in Christ, he is a new creation; the old has gone, the new has come!"

An elephant becoming a butterfly would be no greater miracle! Yes, there is an indescribable miracle that happens inside of us as we live by faith in Jesus. Faith is believing and trusting in God and God alone. It's not a matter of "turning over a new leaf" or just changing some of our old ways of doing things. No, a miracle has happened inside. We know by faith in the Word of God that we are new creations in Jesus Christ. Christianity is walking by faith, not by sight! We know we can hear God speak to us because Christ lives in us.[5]

God's voice matches the character and words of Jesus

One of the basic markers of God's voice is that Jesus Christ is the Living Word of God.[6] We know we are hearing God's voice when we compare what we are hearing with the character, words, spirit and acts of Christ. The supremacy of Jesus is central to hearing from God. In Jesus is the complete totality of God with all His powers and all His attributes. One day before Jesus ascended into heaven, God spotlighted that Jesus is fully God by saying, "This is my Son, whom I love; with him I am well pleased. Listen to him!"[7]

Hebrews 1:2 asserts that God has spoken through His Son. If we want to hear from God, we will follow Jesus and observe His words. We know we are hearing God's voice when it matches the character and words of Jesus. Listen to Him!

God's character shines through

Sometimes we feel we cannot hear from God because we are not righteous enough. But the truth is that Jesus has made us righteous by faith in Him. When God looks at us He sees Jesus first!

> In the Chinese language, the word for "righteousness" is the combination of two pictures. On top is the figure of a lamb; directly beneath is that of a person. What a perfect image of the righteousness that Christ alone provides! Whenever the Father looks at you, He first sees the perfect Lamb of God, "hiding" you. Certainly God is aware of any sin in our lives, but that isn't what He's primarily aware of in any believer. What He sees first and foremost is the beauty of His Son enveloping us.[8]

No matter where you are in your spiritual journey with Christ, God sees the beauty of Jesus in you.

When we know Jesus' character, we can also sense if He is speaking through someone who claims to speak for God. Several years ago when I pastored a church, a visiting speaker gave a specific "word" for me and my leadership team. Our team considered his "word" but did not feel we should do what he was suggesting. The very next day, he called me and gave another "word" even using scripture to pronounce it. Our team met together and united in prayer to receive the Lord's protection because we sensed this action was spiritual manipulation on the part of the speaker. We learned later that this man had brought division and strife to many churches through his "words from God" for them. We knew what the speaker said was not a word from God because it was not compatible with the character of Christ.

God's character reveals His heart

You can have a full life! Christ wants to give us a full, abundant life, and He tells us so when He says "I have come that they might have life, and that they may have it more abundantly."[9]

The word *life* is translated from the Greek word *zoe* which means *the very nature of God and source of life*. The abundant life then, is life filled with the very nature of God inside of us. This life is abundant in quantity and quality—overflowing life. That is the kind of life that God has prepared for us as His children.

As we learn to walk and talk with God over the years, we get to know His heart, His character and His ways. If we are committed to following His character and His ways, He can give us a greater liberty because we become "one with Him." As our spirit becomes filled with His Spirit, and our desires begin to merge with His, we walk in His ways. Jesus said, "I and the Father are one."[10] and "I do nothing on my own but speak just what the Father has taught me."[11] Jesus was one with His Father and was given freedom by His Father on the earth. He knew His heavenly Father so well that He modeled His Father's character and only did what He saw His Father doing.

Hearing God

The Bible says, "Delight yourself in the Lord and he will give you the desires of your heart."[12] This means He puts His desires into our hearts as we follow Him. A friend of mine was involved in politics for many years, but the Lord took the desire away and gave him a heart for mentoring younger leaders. The Lord spoke to him by changing the desires of his heart.

Let's hear Him speak to us by what He reveals through His character that extends to each of us His unconditional love, acceptance, forgiveness and righteousness.

You can hear God through His character

Verses to remember "If we confess our sins, he is faithful and just and will forgive us our sins and purify us from all unrighteousness" (1 John 1:9). "Whoever does not love does not know God, because God is love" (1 John 4:8).

Apply what you've learned
1. How does God reveal His character?
2. How does God reveal Himself through the character and words of Jesus?
3. How can you determine if a desire of your heart is really from God?
4. Has God spoken to you through His character? How?

Chapter Fifteen

God speaks through
Visions and Dreams

God uses visions and dreams to proclaim and reveal His loving guidance to us.

Recently I was in another nation and I saw a vision of a couple walking through a swamp and almost losing each other but coming out on the other side totally clean with the sun shining on them as they walked hand in hand together. As I shared this with them and prayed, they wept. They had been facing difficult times and wondering if they would survive intact. The vision was an affirmation that they would make it through.

Throughout the Bible, God sometimes spoke to His people through visions and dreams. They had the various purposes of directing, consoling, confirming, clarifying, instructing, warning or encouraging God's people. The Bible reveals that visions and dreams are an important part of the latter day outpouring of the Holy Spirit. "In the last days, God says, I will pour out my Spirit on all people. Your sons and daughters will prophesy, your young men will see visions, your old men will dream dreams."[1]

Down through the ages, including the church today, God gives people visions and dreams that clarify their calling or deepen their faith, while giving them a deep assurance from the Lord. Because visions and dreams can be symbolic and thus misinterpreted, many in western Christianity do not take their visions or dreams seriously. Others, like the New Age searchers, look for God in the wrong places without discernment, and get involved in spiritual phenomena that opens them up to the deceptions of Satan.

Just because visions and dreams have caused confusion for some in the body of Christ today does not mean we should dismiss them. We see countless examples in both the Old and New Testaments of people receiving guidance from God through visions and dreams. The Bible tells us that God still speaks through visions and dreams and we must be aware of these "whispers in our ears."

> God speaks again and again, though people do not recognize it. He speaks in dreams, in visions of the night when deep sleep falls on people as they lie in bed. He whispers in their ear...with his warning. He causes them to change their minds; he keeps them from pride.[2]

Visions and dreams from the Lord give us important information that should not be ignored.

How can we discern and recognize God's voice in visions and dreams? First of all, it is important for Christians to be rooted and grounded in the Bible and evaluate every supernatural experience by the Word. We want to be confident that visions and dreams are given for the purpose of guidance or protection and that they glorify our Lord Jesus Christ.

In addition, we need to be in communication with other believers in our local church so we can receive spiritual discernment for our visions and dreams. Consequently, if you have a dream that you believe is God speaking to you but you don't understand it, look for someone who may have the gift of dream interpretation. Joseph, in the book of Genesis, had this gift. An individual with a gift of dream interpretation can help you to discern the imagery found within a dream. For example, free falling in a dream may represent some type of fear in one's life.

With this accountability in place, it helps us to know if a dream or vision is from God.

Visions

Paul the apostle was speaking of his own experience when he revealed to his fellow believers an amazing vision the Lord gave him.

> I must go on boasting. Although there is nothing to be gained, I will go on to visions and revelations from the Lord. I know a man in Christ who fourteen years ago was caught up to the third heaven. Whether it was in the body or out of the body I do not know, God knows. And I know that this man—whether in the body or apart from the body I do not know, but God knows, was caught up to paradise. He heard inexpressible things, things that man is not permitted to tell.[3]

Some believe the Lord gave Paul this vision of heaven that could not be described adequately in human language to strengthen him for his special mission and the exceptional suffering he would endure.

Unlike dreams which occur during our sleep, visions are experiences of intense imagery, sound and feeling occurring during the waking state. There are at least two kinds of visions. One is often referred to as an open vision, which happens when your eyes are open, but you see only the spirit realm instead of your natural surroundings. This is the kind of vision Paul had when he had the vision of heaven. He was so caught up in the vision, he was unaware of his natural surroundings. It almost seemed to him as if he was in paradise itself; it was so real.

God gives supernatural visions that contain important messages for you and others.

These open visions are external views that are like watching a movie. As with visions, God may or may not give you the interpretation. Never presume to know the meaning. Always allow God to reveal it.

Rick Joyner, a prophet from North Carolina has had open visions various times. His book entitled *The Final Quest* describes some of these visions and gives encouragement to the body of Christ.

Another kind of vision you can experience is when you see things "in the spirit." This is a type of impression that the Lord places on your mind and spirit. These impressions or pictures in your mind (mental pictures) are a type of vision the Lord can give to you.

There have been times when I was looking at someone, but in my spirit I was seeing something concerning that person that my natural eyes did not perceive. Sometimes, the Lord may want us to reveal that information to the person, and other times the information was revealed so that we can pray specifically for the individual.

Visions are definitely used by God, but we must be cautious and use wisdom and test the spirits as the Bible instructs us.

> Dear friends, do not believe every spirit, but test the
> spirits to see whether they are from God, because
> many false prophets have gone out into the world.
> This is how you can recognize the Spirit of God:
> Every spirit that acknowledges that Jesus Christ has
> come in the flesh is from God, but every spirit that
> does not acknowledge Jesus is not from God. This is
> the spirit of the antichrist, which you have heard is
> coming and even now is already in the world.[4]

Let me encourage you to always examine both the messenger and the message of a vision. There is a counterfeit for everything, but if you walk in awe of His greatness and power and stay in fellowship with fellow believers, you will know the difference.

One evening I saw a vision in the form of a mental picture. The vision was of a particular couple I knew, and they were standing in a box. I sensed I should share it with them. They admitted that they were feeling like they were restricted in a box. They desperately wanted to move out of the box and into God's destiny for them. My obedience in sharing this vision with them made them realize how much the Lord loves them. It confirmed that He understands how they feel and additionally encouraged them to step out of the confining box they were in.

God speaks in dreams

When God speaks to us through visions, we are awake. When He speaks to us through dreams, they occur while we are asleep. While our body is at rest, our spirit and mind are quite active. We are "thinking" while sleeping. That's why we can wake up with a song on our lips or wake up with feelings of anger.

Dreams are one of the valid ways God can speak to us, but this is also an area in which people can easily get off balance. Most people dream nightly, and their dreams are not all spiritual dreams. Did you ever wake up from a dream and wonder about its meaning, purpose and origin? Sometimes it seems so vivid and real but you are not sure if it was the pizza speaking from a late night snack or if God is trying to speak to you.

God will speak through a dream to reveal Himself to you in a personal way.

The Bible has valued the content of dreams for divine revelation in people's lives down through the ages. Sometimes they were dreams of warning or consolation or guidance. In the Old Testament, God spoke to Joseph in a dream, and Joseph interpreted dreams for Pharaoh, as well as for Pharaoh's servants with whom he was in prison.[5] The Lord spoke to Joseph, the father of Jesus, through a dream, telling him to marry Mary, go to Israel and then to Nazareth in Galilee.[6] Another time, God warned Joseph in a dream to flee to Egypt with baby Jesus and cautioned the wise men to go home a different way.

These dreams had a specific purpose and the message was clear. Those who received the dreams acted in obedience to God. Mary and Joseph fled to Egypt to escape the infanticide ordered by King Herod.[7] The wise men went home on a different route, thus avoiding Herod.

God spoke to my friend Stan one night in a dream to pray for protection for his friends. During the night, he dreamed there was a fire at their house. After he awakened, he prayed for them. A few days later, he heard their grill had exploded. He was certain God had spoken to him in a dream so he would pray for them. Because he had heeded the warning from the dream, there was no damage to their home.

Sometimes dreams are a confirmation of what God has already spoken to us. Jonathan, a young leader of one of our sister churches in Suriname, approached his new fiancée's father to ask permission for his daughter's hand in marriage. Her mother, having never seen Jonathan before, revealed that she saw his face in a dream two months earlier and knew he was going to be the future husband for their daughter, Brigietta.

God sometimes gives dreams to people to console them in life's difficulties. The mother of the early church father, Augustine, was distressed over her then pre-Christian son's immoral lifestyle and begged God for his salvation. The Holy Spirit gave her a dream that showed her worshiping in heaven and to her great joy, there beside her was her son Augustine. She accepted the dream as a promise that Augustine would come to faith in Jesus, which of course he later did.

A dream helped one of my friends during a difficult season in his life. He was involved with a church going through a leadership crisis. Going to church-related activities was challenging, and it was hard for him to sleep. One night he had a dream he was visiting some dear friends who had moved to another country. He woke up with a tremendous sense of peace, and there was almost a tangible presence of the Lord in his bedroom. During this time of stress, God spoke through a dream, and gave him a new sense of serenity and trust in the Lord.

God promised that we would receive dreams in these last days. For most people they are not daily occurrences, although it seems that there are some people who are more prone to opening their spiritual eyes and receiving visions and dreams from the Lord than others.

So how can we tell if it is God's voice in a dream, the enemy's voice in a dream, or the voice of eating dinner too late in a dream? Some dreams are straightforward and clear. We know that they are revealed to clarify something, instruct us, or warn or encourage us in our lives. Some dreams are given to us from the Lord only to alert us to pray and intercede.

A pastor friend says he usually senses if a dream is from God, "Often when I awaken from a dream that seems to have meaning, God's still, small voice is saying, 'That was Me!'" There is an accompanying sense from God that He has spoken.

"Once I dreamed a member of the church was preaching a profound sermon. The moment I awoke I knew I had to write it down. I preached this message the following Sunday! The church member I'd seen in my dream thought it was a very timely word and was stunned when I told him he had "preached" it in my dream!"

We must use caution, however, if dreams confuse us. We should not leap to false conclusions about dream meanings if they are not clear. Some dreams are abstract and cannot be interpreted concretely.

If a dream troubles you, you should discuss it with a trusted mentor or pastor who may be able to give you further insights. There are times when Satan will try to deceive us or cause fear through a dream. If a dream contradicts scripture, it is clearly demonic.

Dreams from God are given to us when God chooses; we should not search for them and make them our focus. Bible teacher Joyce Meyer says, "God doesn't give us dreams to make us feel good or make us more spiritual. Dreams are often interesting to talk about but often are unstable in giving us clear direction for our lives. I have found that people who try to make too much out of their dreams are asking to be deceived."[8] Simply put, God will speak to us in dreams to reveal Himself to us in a personal way, and the dreams will confirm scripture, not contradict it.

Some believers write their dreams down to see if they come to pass. If you are prone to dreams, may I suggest that you maintain a "dream log" placed near your bed so that when awakening in the morning, you can record what you remember. Most of us tend to let the dream escape us if we do not write it down.

Once it is recalled and written, we can then begin to pray over it. Counsel with a trusted friend or spiritual overseer, and await its fulfillment. Often these written journals become needed words of encouragement sometime in the future, and often you may come across someone who reminds you of the dream and suddenly realize it may be a word of encouragement for him.

In conclusion, I encourage you to use discernment, wisdom and balance in hearing God through visions and dreams. If it is God, you will have confirmation in your heart that the Lord is speaking to you or trying to show you something.

You can hear God through visions and dreams

Verse to remember "In the last days, God says, 'I will pour out my Spirit on all people. Your sons and daughters will prophesy, your young men will see visions, your old men will dream dreams'" (Acts 2:17).

Apply what you've learned

1. Why do you think many in Western Christianity do not take their visions and dreams seriously?
2. Has God ever spoken to you through a vision?
3. Why can people get off-balanced when they try to interpret dreams?
4. Has God ever spoken to you through a dream?

Chapter Sixteen

God speaks through
Various Spiritual Gifts

A gift is a sign of relationship. It communicates to others that we appreciate them.

When I give birthday gifts to my children, I give the presents because they are my children and I love them. I do not give them presents because they have been good. I freely and gladly give them gifts because I have a love relationship with them.

Because God longs for a close relationship with us, He freely gives us spiritual gifts that serve as a means of communication— a divine link between us and God. Spiritual gifts are not meant to be mysterious. We are to use spiritual gifts to communicate with the Lord and with others. We can hear God through spiritual gifts! The Lord will often use these gifts to speak to us and to get our attention.

God wants us to understand and use spiritual gifts so we can be both strengthened and involved in service to others. We need each other in order to function effectively for Him. Paul understood this when he told the church at Rome, "I long to see you so that I may impart to you some spiritual gift to make you strong— that is, that you and I may be mutually encouraged by each other's faith."[1]

The Lord has given to His church at least nine different supernatural spiritual gifts:

Now to each one the manifestation of the Spirit is given for the common good. To one there is given through the Spirit the message of wisdom, to another the message of knowledge by means of the same Spirit, to another faith by the same Spirit, to another gifts of healing by that one Spirit, to another miraculous powers, to another prophecy, to another distinguishing between spirits, to another speaking in different kinds of tongues, and to still another the interpretation of tongues. All these are the work of one and the same Spirit, and he gives them to each one, just as he determines.[2]

The first detail we notice about these gifts is that they come from the Holy Spirit. Each one of these gifts is supernatural in nature. They allow us to see, know or do things that we are naturally incapable of accomplishing on our own. God gives us these abilities or gifts that we would have no way of achieving with our natural abilities. For example, although every Christian should be able to pray for healing for those who are ill, some individuals have the healing touch of God flowing through them. This is a supernatural gift of healing. If we use these spiritual gifts in God's way and in His power, not only will we benefit but others will as well.

We also notice in verse 11 that the Holy Spirit gives gifts to "each one," and He decides who will get which gift. Some believers exercise various spiritual gifts.

In this chapter we will look at four of these supernatural spiritual gifts that the Lord uses to speak to us and to others: a message of wisdom, a message of knowledge, discerning of spirits, and spiritual languages.

A message of wisdom

We looked at how God speaks through common sense wisdom in Chapter 13; however, the supernatural spiritual gift of a message of wisdom is not common sense wisdom that has been learned through experience. It is supernatural wisdom that the Lord gives to us when we need it. Paul was exercising a supernatural gift of a message of wisdom when he gave the commander of the ship to Rome guidance regarding navigation in Acts 27. Joseph gave the Pharaoh insights to properly govern Egypt to prepare for the coming famine through supernatural wisdom that the Lord gave to him.

There are times when I am called upon as a consultant and I feel I am "out of my league"; but again and again the Lord gives me supernatural wisdom to pass on to ministry leaders. This wisdom I have not learned through trial and error. It comes from the Lord through a supernatural message of wisdom that allows me to speak appropriate truth at the right

God speaks through a message of wisdom when you need it.

time. Likewise, one of my associates who is marriage counselor is amazed at times when the Lord gives him supernatural wisdom that brings life and healing to marriages. The Lord drops this gift of wisdom into his spirit and he passes it on to those he is counseling. The gift of wisdom will provide them with simple, practical solutions in the midst of conflict.

A message of knowledge

A message of knowledge is a supernatural spiritual gift from the Lord that allows us to discover information that we have not been aware of by any natural means. For example, In Acts 5, Peter received a message of knowledge about Ananias and Sapphira's deception in giving a gift to the church, and the results were quite sobering. God got the instant attention of the entire church!

Many times the Lord uses spiritual gifts to get our attention. One time, God used the gift of a message of knowledge to speak to a wayward young man for whom I was praying. This man had grown up in a Christian home but had backslidden and was addicted to alcohol. He had recently made a commitment to return to the Lord, but was still struggling with a lack of peace in his life.

He and I talked for some time, and then I suggested we spend time praying together. As soon as I closed my eyes and began to pray, I saw a clear mental picture of a liberty bell. It did not make sense to me but I asked him if a liberty bell meant anything to him.

He said it made no sense to him at all. Then he suddenly remembered something. "Come to think of it," he said, "I have continued to drink alcohol in secret and have given the impression that I am free from alcohol. There is a liberty bell on the bottle that I am now drinking."

God speaks through a message of knowledge to reveal information to you.

The Lord supernaturally showed me a liberty bell, a supernatural gift of knowledge that I had no prior information about, to jolt his thinking about an area of secret sin in his life. God got his attention, and today, he is free from his addiction to alcohol.

Discerning of spirits

The Lord also speaks to us through the supernatural gift of discerning of spirits. Some translations of the Bible call this gift "distinguishing between spirits." Sometimes when I walk into a hotel room, I can immediately tell that the room needs to be cleansed of certain evil spirits. I take authority over any unclean spirit and command it to leave in Jesus' name and claim the blood of Jesus over the room. I can almost immediately sense a cleansing taking place in the room.

I minister in a different church nearly every week. Many times, I can discern if there is a spirit of division or a spirit of confusion in the church. No one needs to give any details, the Lord provides this discernment through the spiritual gift of *discerning of spirits.* This helps me to know how to pray and how to more effectively serve this local church.

Did you ever meet a person for the first time and you sense there is something wrong? It may be the Lord is manifesting the gift of discerning of spirits to you so you can respond accordingly. Paul experienced this in Acts when a girl started following him shouting that he was a servant of God. Paul discerned, however, that it was an evil spirit within her that was recognizing God's divine power in him.

God helps you to distinguish, by the discerning of spirits, what He is saying in a particular situation.

> ...We were met by a slave girl who had a spirit by which she predicted the future. She earned a great deal of money for her owners by fortune-telling. This girl followed Paul and the rest of us, shouting, "These men are servants of the Most High God, who are telling you the way to be saved." She kept this up for many days. Finally Paul became so troubled that he turned around and said to the spirit, "In the name of Jesus Christ I command you to come out of her!" At that moment the spirit left her.[3]

Paul discerned that the spirit in the girl was demonic and cast it out. The results of this girl being delivered from an evil spirit opened the door for the gospel to be preached in the city of Philippi.

Spiritual languages

A spiritual gift that is sometimes controversial is called "spiritual languages," or "the gift of tongues."[4] Many believers have received this gift and exercise it in their personal conversations with God as they enter into times of worship and praise. At other times the Lord gives individuals messages in a spiritual language (a language they have not learned) in order to speak to others about the goodness of God.

The Bible describes this kind of spiritual language in Acts 2:

> All of them were filled with the Holy Spirit and began to speak in other tongues as the Spirit enabled them. Now there were staying in Jerusalem God-fearing Jews from every nation under heaven. When they heard this sound, a crowd came together in bewilderment, because each one heard them speaking in his own language. Utterly amazed, they asked: "Are not all these men who are speaking Galileans? **Then how is it that each of us hears them in his own native language?** ...we hear them declaring the wonders of God in our own tongues!" Amazed and perplexed, they asked one another, "What does this mean?"[5]

This miracle of everyone hearing the Lord speak through the apostles and believers in their own language opened the door for Peter to preach the gospel and 3,000 people came to Christ.

Jack Hayford in his book *The Beauty of Spiritual Language* tells the story of sitting on an airplane talking to a businessman who mentioned his Native American ancestry. The Lord prompted Jack to ask the man if he could speak a few words of his spiritual language (tongues). The man was agreeable and Jack spoke aloud a few phrases. The man said it indeed was his tribal language, and Jack was speaking about a Light that had come to the world. Jack, obviously, had never learned this tribal language, but the Lord gave it to him supernaturally. Jack's spiritual language opened the door for him to share the Light of the gospel with the businessman.[6]

God gives messages through spiritual languages to benefit you and others.

120   *Hearing God*

Ron Myer, my associate in ministry for twenty years, was praying in his spiritual language during a prayer time before a church service. A visiting African pastor told Ron later that he was speaking fluently in his native language. Ron had never learned the African language but the Lord gave it to him supernaturally.

Jack Hayford says that the biblical expression of "tongues" often "conjures up strange images in people's minds because they have images of uncontrolled speech or weird gibberish." Hayford maintains that to use the expression "spiritual language" is a more easily accepted description of *tongues speaking* and is precisely biblical.

> The expression "spiritual language" is derived from such references where speaking or singing with tongues is described. The phrases "filled with the Spirit" and "praying...in the Spirit" are the same in the biblical Greek—*en pneumati*. This phrase literally means, "in the spiritual realm and with the Holy Spirit's aid."

> Of course, using the word "spiritual" for this prayer language isn't to suggest that spoken prayer or praise in one's native language is unspiritual or semispiritual. Each form of prayer is at a different dimension, and neither should be described as "less than." How can the Grand Canyon and the Swiss Alps be compared? It's impossible and unnecessary to do so. Rather, be it languages we employ or creation we behold, let us all be humbled before all manifestations of His Majesty's glory. Let us rise together to praise the Creator of all things. To do so is to be open to experiencing the enjoyment and the blessing available in exploring the dimensions to which each realm invites us.[7]

God wants us to have and use spiritual gifts so that we may

be a blessing to others. We need to exercise them so they can be used in our lives to build us up spiritually to give us supernatural strength and ability to be effective in our Christian lives. We should "eagerly desire spiritual gifts."[8]

The gifts are given to serve others, hence no one can claim superiority about any one spiritual gift. All gifts have the purpose of glorifying Christ and benefiting others so we can all hear from God more clearly. God gives you spiritual gifts so you can effectively help your brothers and sisters in Christ hear from heaven.

I have devoted the next chapter to one of the particular gifts—the gift of prophecy—because God often reveals His present and future intentions through prophecy.

You can hear God through various spiritual gifts:
message of wisdom, message of knowledge, discerning of spirits, spiritual languages

Verse to remember

"There are different kinds of gifts, but the same Spirit" (1 Corinthians 12:4).

Apply what you've learned

1. Why does God give us spiritual gifts?
2. Did you ever discern something because God supernaturally revealed it to you?
3. Tell how God has spoken to you in any of the ways mentioned in this chapter.

Chapter Seventeen

God speaks through
Prophecy

The Lord wants to give you a personal message from heaven.

God will speak prophetically with words about the present or the future to impart vision to believers. Carrying a prophetic word in our hearts brings hope.

When the Lord speaks a message through one person for the benefit of another, it is often called a "prophecy." When a prophetic word is given, it is for the purpose of knowing that God will speak directly to you. The Lord will reveal to you that the prophetic word given is a personal message from heaven for you.

About those who prophesy, the Bible says, "…Everyone who prophesies speaks to men for their strengthening, encouragement and comfort."[1] In the Old Testament, prophecy was often given to bring judgment, but in the New Testament it is for strengthening, encouraging and comforting believers.

Prophecy is God giving a personal message from heaven to you.

Sometimes prophecy is foretelling a future event, such as the prophecy Agabus the prophet gave in the book of Acts when he predicted a famine, while at other times it can be a message of encouragement for God's people.

God is a God of the "now." He wants His people to receive a current word from Him so we know what He is saying and doing today. In Chapter 3, we described God's Word as both *logos* and *rhema*. Prophecy is a *rhema* word that sometimes clarifies and emphasizes God's already revealed heart, mind and plans in His *logos* Word. It will never conflict with the written Word; in fact, it often makes the Bible come alive to us.

When God says something prophetically about you, He is speaking out and releasing your potential. God is supernatural, and as Christians, we must by definition be supernatural as well. People today are hungry for the supernatural; you only have to look at the popular books and movies of our day to see this theme of supernatural events or people using supernatural powers. I believe God places this desire for the supernatural in us, yet the enemy is quick to take advantage and produces a counterfeit that draws people away from God, rather than closer to Him.

Prophetic words bring us closer to God

True prophetic words come from God and draw us closer to Him. They are edifying words that God speaks so we can hear Him not only for ourselves but also through others. Sometimes God will use a prophetic word to strengthen and refresh us in our walk with Him. Sometimes we can receive prophetic visions. A woman in our church received this powerful personal prophetic vision for herself while experiencing a time she describes as a "wilderness experience." Here is her story:

> Seemingly everything in my life was being stripped away—parts of my family, many of my friends, and so forth. I wasn't "feeling" the presence of the Lord or hearing His voice much at all. One morning while praying with a dear friend, the Lord gave me a prophetic vision and word. I saw myself standing alone and around my feet was a pile of yarn. It looked like someone had unraveled a sweater around my feet. The Lord showed me that this was a picture of my

life at that moment, but then He clearly spoke that it was from His hand—He was unraveling things that would have bound me up and hindered me. He refreshed my spirit and fortified my resolve to continue to stand in Him.

This prophetic word was a *rhema* word to this woman and served the purpose of encouraging her in a dark time. When God's *rhema* word becomes a reality to us, we realize that God is taking notice and is interested in our circumstances. He has heard us and spoken to us.

God speaks prophetic words through others

In addition to receiving a prophecy directly for oneself, the Lord will also speak to us through a prophecy given by someone else for us. Dr. Bill Hamon defines prophecy as:

> ...simply God communicating His thoughts and intents to mankind. When a true prophecy is given, the Holy Spirit inspires someone to communicate God's pure and exact words to the individual or group for whom they are intended. It is delivered without any additions or subtractions by the one prophesying, including any applications or interpretations suggested by the one speaking. To be most effective, it must also be delivered in God's timing and with the proper spirit or attitude.[2]

The New Testament prophets revealed Jesus through their words of encouragement and insights on coming events, and it is the model for the church today. The Bible gives many examples of prophecies that were spoken to give direction to the people of God.

Agabus the prophet prophesied that if Paul went to Jerusalem he would be bound and delivered to the Gentiles. It happened just as it was prophesied—Paul was arrested and tried in Jerusalem.[3] Timothy received a spiritual gift through a prophetic message when the elders laid their hands on him and prayed for him.[4] Paul told Timothy to wage warfare with prophetic words given to him. "Timothy, my son, I give you this instruction in keeping with the prophecies once made about you, so that by following them you may fight the good fight."[5]

Many times prophecies are confirmations of those things the Lord has already spoken to us in our hearts. At other times the Lord may use prophecy to give us clear direction for our lives. Either way, the prophecy must be in line with the Word of God and our spirits must affirm it.

All prophecy needs to be tested, according to the scriptures. "Do not put out the Spirit's fire; do not treat prophecies with contempt. Test everything. Hold on to the good."[6] Testing a prophecy may mean we go to our pastor or other trusted Christian leader to present it to them and ask for their input. Additionally, all prophecy must be tested by the scriptures. If it does not line up with the Bible, do not receive it.

Prophetic words must have God's timing

We must especially test a prophetic word for timing. It may be for today or it may be for ten years down the road. We must be careful not to assume we know what every personal prophecy means immediately. I learned this the hard way.

Several years ago I had two prophetic messages spoken over me about being called to minister to young people just as I did over two decades ago. One prophetic message came from a pastor in Oregon and the other came from a Presbyterian pastor in New Zealand. I assumed from receiving these two nearly identical prophecies that I was to start a youth ministry, so I did. I began meeting with about 35 youth every week in my hometown.

Shortly thereafter, the Lord also brought me into a relationship with some young leaders who had started a weekly Tuesday Bible study (TBS). As our friendship grew, these leaders started to look to me as one of their spiritual advisors for their fledgling group. While the youth ministry I had started was declining, the TBS youth ministry was growing to over 1,000 young people.

I finally realized that I had missed the timing of God and He never wanted me to start a new youth ministry. He called me to be a mentor to these young leaders. If I had waited to see what God was going to do with TBS, I wouldn't have started the other youth ministry. Timing is always a critical part of seeing a prophetic word come to pass. Getting the wrong timing for prophetic words is the most common error people make in processing prophecy.

Prophetic words must be confirmed in our hearts

Often we are tempted to add to the prophetic word. This usually brings confusion.[7] A friend told me of a prophetic word spoken to his wife and him that said, "I see children." Afterwards, people quickly speculated that they would soon be pregnant since they already had two children. The word never said "pregnancy," and later they saw how they had mentored a teenage mother in their home, like a "daughter."

If somebody tells you through a prophecy to go to the mission field, please don't quit your job unless you know that God has also spoken this same word to you and it is confirmed by the other ways the Lord speaks such as through His peace, circumstances and His still, small voice, for example. I've seen people get into horrible problems by trying to run their lives based on what other people told them was a "prophetic message from God."

If the prophecy you receive doesn't bear agreement in your heart, you often will know it by a lack of peace in your spirit. Something tells you things just are not quite right.

There are a lot of well-meaning people who think they are hearing from God for others, but the truth is they are not. If someone prophesies something to you that is not already in your heart, then I suggest you write down the words that are spoken over you and wait for the Lord to reveal to you whether or not the words are from Him. If it is from God, He will clearly show you.

Allow God to speak to you prophetically

The Lord desires to place His words in our mouths and speak through us prophetically to others. Jesus promises to "…give you words and wisdom that none of your adversaries will be able to resist or contradict."[8] If the Lord speaks a message in your spirit that you believe is a true prophecy for someone else, be careful not to be presumptuous when giving it to the individual. As much as is possible, try to have the individual's spiritual leaders involved in this process so they can help the person discern the meaning of the prophecy.

When I have given an individual a prophetic message, I usually have said something like: "I sense the Lord may be saying… rather than "thus says the Lord." We often turn people off by our super-spiritual mannerisms, our traditions or by our personalities. I sometimes encounter older ministers who prophesy in King James English. It is unclear to me why someone getting a word from God would chose to speak like they did during the King James era; however, perhaps it is best to look beyond the language used and the vessel God has chosen in order to concentrate on the word of the Lord.

I was told years ago that a prophecy is like a clear, clean refreshing stream of water from the Lord; however, the channel or person who gives the prophetic message is like a hose. So we should not be surprised when we encounter a problem: the prophecy may taste a bit like the hose! We must discern between the message from the Lord and the hose—the person giving the message.

I believe God wants us to be encouraged with prophecies that help us to know Him better. We can trust that as His sheep, we will learn to recognize His voice, all the while remembering that prophecy is just one of the ways God speaks to us and should not be used exclusively to hear from God. Nevertheless, let's continue to seek Him and keep our hearts open as He speaks prophetic words that help refresh our walk with Him.

You can hear God through prophecy

Verse to remember
"Do not treat prophecies with contempt.
Test everything. Hold on to the good"
(1 Thessalonians 5:20-22).

Apply what you've learned
1. How can you determine if a prophecy spoken over you is true or not?
2. Why is timing so important for prophetic words?
3. Tell of any time the Lord gave a prophecy to you or for someone else.

Chapter Eighteen

God speaks through
A Daily Encounter

Daily time set aside to meet with God should be like a visit with your closest friend.

We make time for close friends and look forward to their visits. The Lord cherishes time with us too. He is a God of relationship. He created us with a desire to have close and intimate relationships. First and foremost, we were created to have a relationship with Him and then with one another.

Why is it so vitally important for every believer to have a daily time alone with God? Although we may "pray without ceasing" and walk with the Lord minute by minute, designating a special time of day to be alone with the Lord is vital to relating heart-to-heart with God. It helps to give a divine rhythm to our daily routine as we place ourselves in a position to hear from God.

I have a great relationship with my wife, and we often communicate through cell phone or in personal contact many times throughout the day; however, she still appreciates a special night when we can spend time alone together without distractions. We call it our "date

You have the opportunity to wait and listen during a daily encounter with God.

night," and keep that regular appointment even though we have been married for over three decades. Making time with God a daily priority is saying that our relationship with the Lord is important and therefore we will set apart concentrated time to build this relationship.

Yet so frequently, as Christians we find it hard to commit to a daily time with God. Often, we fall into a rut of allowing our time to become a drudgery or an obligation.

Max Lucado writes that because some of us have tried and not been successful, we practice a type of surrogate spirituality where we rely on others to spend time with God and try to benefit from their experience.

> Let them tell us what God is saying. After all, isn't that why we pay preachers? Isn't that why we read Christian books? These folks are good at daily devotions. I'll just learn from them. If that is your approach, if your spiritual experiences are secondhand and not firsthand, I'd like to challenge you with this thought: Do you do that with other parts of your life? I don't think so.
>
> You don't do that with vacations. You don't say, "Vacations are such a hassle, packing bags and traveling. I'm going to send someone on vacation for me. When he returns, I'll hear all about it and be spared all the inconvenience." Would you do that? No! You want the experience firsthand. You want the sights firsthand, and you want to rest firsthand. Certain things no one can do for you.[1]

The simple fact remains—if we truly want an intimate, grace-filled relationship with God, we have to spend time alone with Him on a regular basis. Listening to God is a firsthand experience.

A listening room

Ralph Neighbour suggests that our meeting time with God should involve so much more than a one-way conversation in which we speak to God. He says, "It also involves listening to Him, and everyone needs a listening room where we can hear the directions of God for our own needs, the needs of others and for His assignments to us."

> A Japanese pastor invited an American pastor to visit his home. The Japanese pastor took his guest to a lovely garden behind the house, where a one-room cottage stood. The pastor explained, "This is my 'listening room.'"
>
> Our "listening room" is more an attitude, a value of our lives, than a special room built for that purpose. It is a condition in which we not only speak to Him, but also hear from Him. God does speak![2]

When we spend time listening for God to speak, He will! Our daily encounters with God place us in a position to seek Him on behalf of not only our own needs but the needs of others as well. We are part of the body of Christ, and our priestly task is to pray and intercede for others. Ralph says that "in these daily 'listenings' we become the priest of God, bringing the body members before Him and coming away with edification for our fellow members." Our alone time with God gives us the opportunity to hear Him speak so that we can be encouraged and we can in turn encourage others.

What works for you?

Avoiding legalistic approaches to spending time with the Lord will help us to keep the time fresh and inviting. First of all, we should never allow others' expectations to manipulate our emotions and make us feel guilty for not devoting an hour or two alone with God each day. Although some people will easily spend an hour or more each day with God, others may have to start at five, ten or fifteen minutes, and increase it over time. Allow the peace of God to rule in your heart about the time you believe God wants you to spend with Him. The best length of time spent with God is the time you will actually practice! Start with a realistic goal.

If you want your encounters to stay fresh, you cannot do it out of legalism but instead because you hear God calling you each day saying, "Arise, my love...and come away...."[3] If you miss a day or so, God is not disappointed in you. He always welcomes you back with open arms. He is thrilled when you seek a friendship with Him.

You should pick the time of day that works for you. It works best for me to spend time alone with the Lord in the morning. I find that I am most alert and can give God my peak concentration in the morning; but everyone is different. So find the time, readjust your priorities and plan for it.

Two main activities of spending time with God are reading the Bible and prayer. The Bible is God speaking to humanity. Reading the Bible opens the door to communication from God. I use a Bible reading plan[4] that takes me through the Bible at my own pace.

Trying to listen for God's voice without being dedicated to spending time in God's Word on a regular basis will open us up to hearing voices that are not from the Lord. Knowing the written Word of God protects us from deception. There are many evil spirits ready to whisper lies to us if we are not prepared spiritually by studying the Word of God.

Knowledge of the Word is of vital importance to us in discerning the voice of God. If we don't know the Word, we won't have anything with which to compare the ideas and arguments that war against God's perfect will for our lives. The devil can give us ideas that may make sense to us, but just because something seems logical does not necessarily mean it is from God. We may hear what we want to hear, but it doesn't mean we have heard from God. An idea can feel good to our emotions but fail to give us lasting peace when it isn't in line with God's Word.

A quiet nudge from the Lord

Barbara often discovered that God spoke to her about something specific during her early morning quiet time. One morning, she felt a strong urge to go look under the eaves of her attic bedroom. She thought to herself, "I don't think I am just being distracted, I think this really is the Lord speaking to me. Besides, I've just showered and getting on my hands and knees to crawl into the dusty attic space is not something I would think to do myself!"

She decided to be obedient to this nudge from the Lord, and discovered a large china set there she had forgotten about. She decided to give it to her aunt who was looking for more dishes for her growing family. The timing was perfect.

Her aunt had just written in her journal to God the day before about how hard it was giving up pretty things like dishes because of the twenty years she and her husband had spent on the mission field. When she heard that she would get a lovely set of dishes, she trembled with joy at hearing God speak in this specific way. God loves to encourage us and affirm that He cares about the details of our lives. Not only was Barbara encouraged to listen and hear further from God during her quiet times, God answered her aunt's heart desires by showing her that He really does care.

Prayer is simply talking with God. It is a two-way conversation between you and God. When you spend time alone with a friend you start to understand your friend's hopes, dreams and wants. You do this by speaking and by taking time to listen to your friend. Communication is incomplete if all you do is talk.

The more listening time you spend with your heavenly Father, the better you will understand His heart for you. Do not expect God to function simply as a drive-through fast food restaurant. While we may place our order (heart's desire), we must take time to hear His heart's desire on the matter. God always knows what is best and always has the timing exact.

God seeks to quiet the noise in order to make way for His voice to be heard. When is the last time you got away for an extended period of time without technology at your fingertips, where you just sat and quieted yourself by the beach, or simply closed the door and sat in silence waiting on God? Too often life is such a rush that we rush up to God, say a few hurried prayers and rush away again.

A young man who was struggling with his newfound faith told me once that he did not like it quiet because God would speak to him during those times, convicting him of things in his life that he needed to change.

To hear God's voice, we must learn to find ways to be quiet and listen for the Lord to speak. We must fix our eyes on Jesus and worship Him and Him only without distractions. The Bible says that Jesus departed to a lonely place to pray early in the morning,[5] and after a day's ministry, He went to a mountain to pray and be alone with God.[6]

As you talk to God and spend a quiet time listening, you can draw on His presence and power to give your spiritual life energy and vitality. You will begin to understand Him and know what He wants you to do.

There is a story told of a man who in utter frustration asked his pastor why God had not been giving him answers. Unable to hear the pastor's mumbled reply, the man moved closer, asking the pastor to repeat what he had said. Still unable to hear the reply, he moved closer and closer until finally his ear almost touched the pastor. Then he heard in the faintest voice, "Sometimes God whispers so that we will move closer to Him."

God desires our closeness. He wants our unwavering love. Developing a love relationship with the Lord changes us from the depths of our beings. We will learn to hear His voice more clearly when we spend time with Him. Let God have all of you as you develop a listening heart that is open to hear His whispers.

Hearing God
through a daily encounter

Verse to remember "Blessed is the man who listens to me, watching daily at my doors..." (Proverbs 8:34).

Apply what you've learned

1. Do you have a listening room? What do you do there?
2. How do you keep your time with God each day from becoming an obligation?
3. Discuss ways God speaks to you in your daily encounter with Him.

Chapter Nineteen

God speaks through
Journaling

A way to enrich your quiet time with the Lord and hear His voice is through journaling.

Journaling is writing down what is in your heart—your thoughts, prayers, fears, disappointments, joys and miracles in your life. Sometimes you may record a scripture that God quickens to you. Did you ever experience a verse almost leaping off the pages of the Bible during a time alone with God? You may have read it one thousand times, but this time it really "grabs" you. God is speaking to you! Write it down so you do not lose it when you need it most. Proverbs says, "Treasure my commandments within you...Write them on the tablet of your heart."[1]

I've heard someone say that the only thing required of journaling is honesty. Journaling is like keeping a spiritual diary. Writing down your honest thoughts and God's responses to your requests, thoughts, feelings and insights provides a way of remembering God's activity in your life. A journal helps you to look back over time and see a written record of the Lord's dealings with your life.

When the prophet Habakkuk needed an answer from the Lord, the Lord replied by

God speaks through journaling, recording what He quickens to your heart.

mentioning the importance of writing down what He said to him and waiting for a reply.

> I will stand at my watch and station myself on the
> ramparts; I will look to see what he will say to me,
> and what answer I am to give to this complaint. Then
> the Lord replied: "Write down the revelation and
> make it plain on tablets so that a herald may run with
> it. For the revelation awaits an appointed time; it
> speaks of the end and will not prove false. Though it
> linger, wait for it; it will certainly come and will not
> delay."[2]

Habakkuk was a prophet who was seeking to hear God speak. First he went to a quiet place where he would be alone and wait for God to speak. He listens and "looks to hear what God will say." When God begins to speak, he tells Habakkuk to record the vision that he is sensing in his heart. God clearly showed His prophet how to dialogue with Him by using the combination of coming to a quiet place, listening and journaling.

Write it down so you don't lose it!

Writing what God is speaking to you becomes a reminder of the revelation God has given you that has not yet come to pass. When the Lord speaks to me, I write it down so I do not lose it. There are things God spoke to me more than 20 years ago that are only now coming to pass. And those revelations often look much different than I expected. If I had not written them down, I would no longer have them to help guide me into what God has for me today.

Journaling is really a method to be used to help you learn to discern God's voice better. In *Communion With God*, Mark and Patti Virkler believe one of the greatest benefits of using a journal during time spend with the Lord is that it allows you "to receive freely the spontaneous flow of ideas that come to your mind, in faith believing that they are from Jesus, without short-circuiting them by subjecting them to rational and sensory doubt." Mark further explains it like this:

> I found that before I began keeping a journal, I would ask God for an answer to a question, and as soon as an idea come into my mind, I would immediately question whether the idea was from God or from self; and, in so doing, I was short-circuiting the intuitive flow of the Spirit by subjecting it to rational doubt. I would get one idea from God and doubt that it was from Him, and therefore get no more. Now, by writing it down, I can receive whole pages in faith, knowing I will have ample time to test it later. Maintaining a journal keeps your mind occupied (therefore, out of the way) and on track as you are receiving God's words.[3]

Some people object to journaling because they compare it to Satan's counterpart—automatic writing. Journaling is not to be confused with demonically inspired automatic writing which allows you to be overtaken by a spirit that controls your hand to write down what a voice is telling you. Instead, biblical journaling comes from the flow of ideas birthed by God in your heart and then writing those thoughts down with a hand under your own control. These spontaneous thoughts, feelings and impressions should always be tested and examined later to be sure they line up with scripture.

Journaling is a written record of God's words to you

Journaling is really just a written record of how God has been working in your life. God may speak to you about something today that you may need ten years down the road. It is a way to look back over the years and see how God has been faithful to hear and answer your prayers and discover how you have grown spiritually. It is a way of holding yourself accountable to move on to spiritual maturity.

Journaling can be a form of meditative worship. Alone with God, we can explore our passion for the Lord as we write what is on our hearts to God.

You can use a simple spiral bound notebook or a fancier hardbound journal to keep track of your impressions, inspired thoughts and scriptures as you write down what God is speaking to you. Your journal could even be your computer where you type your thoughts during your quiet time with God. I have heard of some who use tape recorders to record the thoughts coming to them during their time with God. Any of these methods of keeping track of hearing from God are valuable ones.

Cultivating an ever-deepening relationship with the Lord through journaling helps you to clearly think through what you believe the Lord is speaking to you about. You can test it with the scriptures and read it from time to time to see how your mind, heart and spirit have been renewed by the Lord. You will discover that you have learned how to converse with God as you focus the eyes of your heart on God and receive fresh words from Him each day.

Hearing God through journaling

Verse to remember: "Write down the revelation and make it plain on tablets...For the revelation awaits an appointed time; it speaks of the end and will not prove false. Though it linger, wait for it; it will certainly come and will not delay" (Habakkuk 2:2-3).

Apply what you've learned
1. Describe what journaling is in your own words.
2. Why is it important to test what you write?
3. Do you record God's activity in your life through journaling? Discuss answers to prayer that you have received.

Hearing God

Chapter Twenty

God speaks through
Prayer and Fasting

Prayer is communicating in intimate conversation with God.

Regardless of the different ways God communicates with us, He often speaks to us in response to prayer. Psalm 91:15 says that when we call on Him, He will answer. Although we have been discussing how God speaks to us in answer to prayer already throughout this book, let's take a closer look at how it affects our everyday lives. Cornell Haan, co-founder of the World Prayer Team, recalls how his mother would be sitting in her chair praying when, as a rebellious teenager, he arrived home after curfew.

> She did not scold me or punish me, but simply sat there, often with tears in her eyes, praying for me. It caused me to be very ashamed of my disobedience— more so than a sharp talking to or being grounded. From her I learned to pray about problems more and to speak harshly less.[1]

God heard and answered this mother's prayers, and her son's life was changed. Our prayers keep us on God's mind. They cause God to notice our heartfelt supplications.

God speaks in response to your prayers.

God spoke to Cornelius in the book of Acts in response to

his sincere prayers. "Four days ago I was in my house praying at this hour, at three in the afternoon. Suddenly a man in shining clothes stood before me and said, 'Cornelius, **God has heard your prayer** and remembered your gifts to the poor. Send to Joppa for Simon who is called Peter.'"[2]

Cornelius, a Gentile, who was not yet a believer in Jesus Christ, had a generous heart. He prayed and God noticed and spoke to him. He sent an angel to tell Cornelius to invite a Jewish stranger to his home who would tell him about Jesus. God loves to answer us when we pray sincere prayers to Him.

The parents of John the Baptist, heard God speak in answer to their prayers. "Then an angel of the Lord appeared to him, standing at the right side of the altar of incense. When Zechariah saw him, he was startled and was gripped with fear. But the angel said to him: 'Do not be afraid, Zechariah; **your prayer has been heard**. Your wife Elizabeth will bear you a son, and you are to give him the name John.'"[3]

Jesus tells two stories in the book of Luke that emphasize the importance of continuing a determined perseverance in prayer. In the first story He says:

> Suppose one of you has a friend, and he goes to him at midnight and says, "Friend, lend me three loaves of bread, because a friend of mine on a journey has come to me, and I have nothing to set before him." Then the one inside answers, "Don't bother me. The door is already locked, and my children are with me in bed. I can't get up and give you anything." I tell you, though he will not get up and give him the bread because he is his friend, yet because of the man's boldness he will get up and give him as much as he needs.

Just as this man gave in after repeated requests from his friend, so our God will respond after persistent prayer. Jesus went on to say: "Ask and it will be given to you; seek and you will find; knock and the door will be opened to you. For everyone who asks receives; he who seeks finds; and to him who knocks, the door will be opened."[4]

We must ask in order to receive an answer. When we seek Him, we find Him. When we continue to knock, God will answer. The Bible tells us we do not have, because we do not ask.[5]

If we feel we seldom hear from God, perhaps we have stopped asking. If we draw near to Him, He will draw near to us.[6] He is waiting for us to make the next move. He already made His move toward us when He sent Jesus to the cross 2.000 years ago.

Jesus told His disciples a second story:

> In a certain town there was a judge who neither feared God nor cared about men. And there was a widow in that town who kept coming to him with the plea, "Grant me justice against my adversary." For some time he refused. But finally he said to himself, "Even though I don't fear God or care about men, yet because this widow keeps bothering me, I will see that she gets justice, so that she won't eventually wear me out with her coming!" And the Lord said... "And will not God bring about justice for his chosen ones, who cry out to him day and night?"[7]

God loves to answer our prayers. But at times, we need to persevere and continue to ask until we receive the answer. Just this week I received a major answer to prayer. The international leadership team that I lead had been praying for years for the Lord to provide a property we could purchase for our international ministry. We rented facilities for many years and really desired to have a building of our own. This week, after years of perseverance, the Lord opened the door for us to purchase a facility that is a perfect fit for our ministry. It pays to persevere.

There are times when prayer should be accompanied with fasting

Prayer and fasting go hand-in-hand. Fasting is a discipline of intercession that carries the potential for answered prayer. When we fast and intercede, we pray and expect God to answer.

What is fasting exactly? When we fast, we are abstaining from daily nourishment for a period of time. We "starve" our bodies in order to feed our spirits. The essence of a fast is self-denial in order to turn our thoughts to God. We can hear God's voice more clearly when we fast because we find in Him a sustenance beyond food. When prayer and fasting is combined, powerful things happen.

In Mark 9, Jesus healed a boy with an evil spirit. The disciples asked Jesus afterwards, "Why could we not cast him [the evil spirit] out?" Jesus replied, "This kind can come out only by prayer and fasting."[8] Jesus was challenging His disciples to be prayed up and maintain a life of prayer and fasting so that their faith remained firm.

Jesus does not mean that a time of prayer was necessary before

The self-denial of fasting increases your capacity to hear from God.

this kind of evil spirit could be driven out. Rather, a principle is implied here: where there is little faith, there is little prayer. Where there is much prayer [and fasting], founded on true commitment to God and his Word, there is much faith. Had the disciples been maintaining as Jesus did, a life of prayer, they could have dealt successfully with this case.[9]

Maintaining a life of prayer and fasting is paramount to hearing from God. Many times my associates and I have heard the voice of God in a significant way while engaged in a season of fasting. One associate, who gets numerous speaking engagements, makes the decision about which ones to take during a time of fasting. All the invitations seem good, but which ones does the Lord really want him to accept? It is especially important for him to know the ones to take when extensive traveling is involved. He makes the final decision during times of fasting because fasting sharpens his hearing.

Fasting is not an option for Christians who are serious about their walk with God. One time as Jesus was teaching on prayer and fasting, He used the term, "When you fast..."[10] and went on and made His point. Notice, he did not say, "If you fast...." Jesus knew that fasting would open up a whole new realm of revelation for Christians and make it easier for them to hear the voice of the Holy Spirit.

In addition to increasing our capacity to receive from the Lord, fasting has a way of quieting all the background noise of life so we can tune in to His voice.

I know of a family who found the Lord's direction for housing during fasting. Cathy and her family had been casually looking for housing for some time. While she was on an extended fast, she spoke to a lady at the hairdressers who was selling a home privately at a very reasonable price. It turned out the home was almost an exact fit for Cathy's family.

She and her husband sensed it was the Lord's direction for them to move and they bought it. They could move into the new house within two months, but they needed to sell their current house first. Cathy's husband was on an extended fast, and together they felt the house would be sold shortly. Indeed, the house was sold at a favorable price, with much more money than they expected to get, on day six of his fast.

In the book of Acts, we find the early church receiving direction from the Lord as they were fasting. In Antioch there was a group of church leaders who were worshiping the Lord and fasting when the Holy Spirit spoke to them about commissioning Barnabas and Paul and sending them on a trip to preach the gospel.[11] This trip later became known as Paul's first missionary trip that took Christianity to areas that previously had not heard the gospel.

On this trip, Paul and Barnabas experienced many miracles, saw a large number of new converts and planted new churches. When it was time to appoint leaders for those churches, how do you think they heard from God about who the leaders should be? It was through prayer and fasting.[12]

Leadership selection is a major decision in a church. If fasting should be involved in major decisions in the church, then it should certainly be involved in major decisions in our lives. If you are considering marriage, changing jobs, changing careers, or other significant life decisions, it is to your advantage to include fasting in your decision-making process.

I love the story of Daniel. He had fasted for a period of three weeks when an angel appeared to him and said, "Since the first day that you set your mind to gain understanding...I have come in response....I have come to explain to you what will happen..."[13] Daniel had a question that he was asking the Lord, and the answer came as he was fasting. I sometimes like to call this the missing piece of the puzzle. God showed Moses the pattern for the tabernacle on the mountain during fasting. Queen Esther instructed her Jewish brethren to fast for three days and three nights before she appeared before the king in order to plead for the lives of her people. God answered by giving her favor with the king. The Bible is filled with examples of godly men and women receiving direction from the Lord as a result of fasting.

A friend of mine had been asking the Lord for a long time about how to walk the fine line between holiness and legalism. It was during a season of seeking the Lord via fasting that he received the missing piece of scriptural insight that he needed from the Lord. He now is quite confident that he has the revelation of how to walk in victory in this area of his life.

Although I believe we are all called to fast at certain times, we must avoid legalistic approaches to fasting. God gives grace for some individuals to fast for longer periods of time and others for shorter times. If you have never fasted before, ask God for His grace to experience the blessing of fasting. Start by missing a few meals or fast for a day or two. Some Christians fast for a few meals or a day each week. Be sure to drink water or juices when you fast. There are many good books that you can read that give a balanced approach to biblical fasting.[14]

What if you fast and the Lord does not speak to you in a significant way? This really is the wrong question to ask. What if you fast and He does speak to you? We know it is His will for us to fast, so we can trust that He will honor our obedience as we seek His voice through prayer and fasting.

Hearing God through prayer and fasting

Verse to remember "But when you fast, put oil on your head and wash your face, so that it will not be obvious to men that you are fasting, but only to your Father, who is unseen; and your Father, who sees what is done in secret, will reward you" (Matthew 6:17-18).

Apply what you've learned
1. Why is it important to continue in perseverance in prayer?
2. How do prayer and fasting go hand-in-hand?
3. When should prayer be accompanied by fasting?
4. Give some examples when the Lord spoke to you through your times of prayer and fasting.

Chapter Twentyone

God speaks through
Angels

The Bible tells us that God sends angels at times to deliver messages to His people.

God speaking through such a supernatural occurrence is a more uncommon way for us to hear God, but when angels speak we should listen to what they say.

God can and will speak to us in every way that He has spoken in the past. I choose to believe God speaks through angels, because of the clear evidence in the Bible which I believe to be the true Word of God.

Today's culture is fascinated with the topic of angels because it is searching for supernatural and spiritual meaning. We have TV shows, magazine articles and books taking the topic of angels

Hearing through an angel is a more uncommon way God speaks to you, but it can happen.

quite seriously, but most reveal a very poor grasp of what the Bible really teaches about angels. This only adds to the confusion of who holy angels really are and what they do.

Angels are messengers of God

Angels are servants of God and are described in Hebrews as spirits "to help and care for those who are to receive his salvation."[1] They are God's messengers to protect, provide, proclaim God's truth or carry out God's judgments. They are spiritual beings created by God to serve Him and man.

Let me begin by saying there are many, many incidences of angels appearing in the Bible. In both the Old and the New Testament angels were commonplace. Many times angels appeared to guide, comfort and provide for God's people as they performed certain tasks. Sometimes they intervened in the affairs of nations or helped people in times of suffering or persecution.

An angel shut the lions' mouths when Daniel was thrown into their den. An angel appeared to Mary telling her she would bear a son. An angel rolled away the stone from Jesus' tomb. Cornelius was visited by an angel who told him to send for Peter. As a result, Peter was instrumental in leading Cornelius and his whole household to Christ.

Fallen angels do not speak for God

Although holy angels are the messengers of God, the Bible tells us there are also other angels—demons of darkness. God's holy angels remain obedient to God and carry out His will, but the fallen angels fell from their holy position and now try everything to thwart God's purposes here on earth. In his book *Angels*, Billy Graham describes how some of God's created angels fell:

> Few people realize the profound part angelic forces play in human events…. Satan, or the devil, was once called "Lucifer, the song of the morning."…When the angel Lucifer rebelled against God and His works, some have estimated that as many as one third of the angelic hosts of the universe may have joined him in his rebellion. Thus, the war that started in heaven continues on earth and will see its climax at Armageddon with Christ and His angelic army victorious.[2]

God's holy angels war against the fallen angels on our behalf. As I mentioned earlier in this book, Joseph Smith the founder of the Mormons, experienced a deceptive angel of darkness,[3] not one of God's angels. The devil, we are told in the Bible, masquerades as an angel of light.[4] This is why we need to know the Word of God, so we can discern between the real and the counterfeit.

Regardless of our culture's fascination with angels, we should never contact angels, pray to them, or worship them. In addition to not contradicting the Bible, any action of holy angels will glorify God and be consistent with His character.

How angels intervene to help, comfort and protect us

If you are a Christian, according to the Bible, you have angels looking out for you. God created angels to help accomplish His work in this world, and they watch over Christians and will assist us because we belong to God. Psalm 91:11 says, "For he will command his angels concerning you to guard you on all your ways."

Former President Ronald Reagan's daughter relates the story of visiting her father in the hospital after he was shot soon after his inauguration. Apparently, he saw angels surrounding him during this critical time after surgery.

> My mother told me that he woke up at one point after the doctors had operated on him, unable to talk because there was a tube down his throat. He saw figures in white standing around him and scrawled on a piece of paper, "I'm alive, aren't I?"...I repeated [the story] to a friend—a nurse—who pointed out to me that no one in a recovery room or in intensive care is in white; they're all in green scrubs....I give endless prayers of thanks to whatever angels circled my father, because a Devastator bullet, which miraculously had not exploded, was finally found a quarter inch from his heart. Without divine intervention, I don't know if he would have survived.[5]

When Peter was released from prison by an angel and arrived at the door of Mary's house, the believers meeting there could not believe it was Peter in person but said, "It must be his [guardian] angel."[6] Jesus had told His followers earlier that those with childlike faith would have the services of angels, "...their angels have constant access to my Father."[7] As a believer, God provides angels for you because He loves you and will speak comfort and protection to you through these messengers.

You may not be aware of the presence of angels around you and you cannot predict how they will appear. This explains the verse in the Bible that says, "Do not forget to entertain strangers, for by so doing some people have entertained angels without knowing it."[8] Just because you have never seen an angel does not mean angels are not present with you. My wife is convinced that I have many angels who protect me while I drive, because I often get so preoccupied while driving that I need supernatural intervention to keep the car on the road!

Although angels are spirits, they make themselves visible when needed. There have been angelic sightings all over the world. I have a close relative who saw an angel in her bedroom to bring her comfort and hope during a time of great need. She told me a deep peace came over her when she had the angelic visitation.

A friend of mine was detained in Albania many years ago for handing out Bibles. Miraculously she and her friend were released. The only problem was that they were out in the middle of nowhere, each with a heavy suitcase. It was miles to the Yugoslavian border. Miraculously, a man stopped and offered to drive them through the countryside and straight to the border. He dropped them off and was gone, returning the way he had come. They were convinced it was an angel who had provided help in their time of need.

John G. Paton, pioneer missionary in the New Hebrides Islands, told a thrilling story involving the protective care of angels. Hostile natives surrounded his mission headquarters one night, intent on burning the Patons out and killing them. The Patons prayed all during the terror-filled night that God would deliver them. When daylight came they were amazed to see that, unaccountably, the attackers had left. They thanked God for delivering them.

A year later, the chief of the tribe was converted to Jesus Christ, and Mr. Paton, remembering what had happened, asked the chief what had kept him and his men from burning down the house and killing them. The chief replied in surprise, "Who were all those men you had with you there?" The missionary answered, "There were no men there; just my wife and I." The chief argued that they had seen many men standing guard—hundreds of big men in shining garments with drawn swords in their hands. They seemed to circle the mission station so that the natives were afraid to attack. Only then did Mr. Paton realize that God had sent His angels to protect them.[9]

Many Christians can recall those times when they were in danger and were miraculously spared. Could it be that, although they saw no angels, their presence helped avert tragedy? Is God trying to get our attention and remind us of His goodness to us?

Even if we never see an angel physically, we should be aware of how close God's ministering angels are and sense their presence so we can face each day, trusting God to care for us. Moreover, be sure to be kind to strangers; they could be angels sent from God to speak to you!

Hearing God through angels

Verse to remember "Are not all angels ministering spirits sent to serve those who will inherit salvation?" (Hebrews 1:14).

Apply what you've learned
1. Explain how angels are God's messengers.
2. What is their purpose for appearing to humans?
3. Have you or anyone you know ever had an encounter with an angel giving a message from God?

Chapter Twentytwo

God speaks through
Surprises

God loves to surprise us.

For those of us who remember the 1960's Andy Griffith Show, we recall fondly imitating, along with millions of other television viewers, the familiar refrain of the likeable Gomer Pyle, "Surprise! Surprise! Surprise!" delivered in a Southern drawl. His enthusiasm for surprises was contagious and joyous.

Anyone in a long-distance relationship knows that hearing a friend's voice over the telephone unexpectedly is a welcomed sound. Fresh communication is important for any relationship. God will sometimes surprise us through an unexpected revelation from Him. By now, it should not surprise us that God has many, many options to speak to us.

Sometimes God will surprise us and speak through something we would never expect. For example, there is a story in the Bible of the Lord speaking through a donkey to Balaam the prophet.[1] At the time, Balaam was out of the will of God and trying to walk through a door the Lord had closed to him. So the Lord sent an angel to block Balaam and his donkey from continuing on. The donkey saw the angel, but Balaam did not. That is, until he beat the donkey to try to make it move, and the Lord caused the donkey to talk! Not

God may surprise you with a fresh revelation.

only were Balaam's ears opened, but his eyes were opened as well. He saw an angel with his sword drawn in their path. God rebuked the greedy prophet in this quite unusual way to keep him from making a serious mistake. Sometimes God's surprises will keep us from making the wrong move in our lives.

God speaks through an audible voice

Although rare, God may even surprise us by speaking through an audible voice. God's people in both the Old and New Testaments on occasion heard His literal, audible words. We know about Adam, with whom God walked in the Garden of Eden. God also spoke audibly to the prophets, the patriarchs and Noah.

In the New Testament, people heard God's literal voice on a few occasions. Peter, James and John heard God's voice during the transfiguration. God spoke to Jesus at His baptism. The moment Jesus came up out of the water at His baptism, a voice from heaven said, "This is my Son, whom I love; with him I am well pleased."[2]

In Acts 9, at Paul's conversion on the Damascus road, Christ spoke directly to him, and those around him also heard Jesus speaking.

It is interesting to note, however, that although the Acts 9 account mentions that others also heard, in Acts 22 when Paul is describing his conversion experience, he says those with him "saw the light but did not hear the voice of the one who was speaking to me." Bible scholars attribute this seeming contradiction to the Greek translation of the word "hear" in the first account which actually means they "heard something without understanding." When Paul describes his experience later, he is referring to the fact that those with him did not "discern" the voice of the Lord. They heard the sound, but couldn't make out what was being said.

A similar occurrence takes place when Jesus was teaching one day and God spoke audibly.[3] Although the disciples heard God's audible voice and understood exactly what He spoke, some people heard God's voice as "thunder" and some thought an angel spoke. Apparently most people did not hear discernible language but only sound of some kind.

How could people hear the same voice and hear it differently? Could it be that it depended on the spiritual state of the person hearing? Not everyone was in a spiritual position to hear the voice as God's. Some probably thought it was just their imaginations.

Not surprisingly, it is important for us not only to hear, but to hear with understanding. It is quite possible that to hear God's audible voice, we must be in a position to hear it. Our hearts must be open to hear God, just as little Samuel's was when he finally recognized the voice he was hearing as God's and responded in childlike faith, "Speak, I'm listening." In other words, it is easier to discern God's voice when we are in a close relationship with the Lord, like Samuel who "continually ministered before the Lord."

God speaks through a non-Christian

It may surprise you, but God can also speak through unsaved people to get your attention. God spoke through a heathen king of Egypt to send a message to the godly King Josiah, telling him not to go to battle. King Josiah ignored this pagan's claim to be hearing from God; he went to war anyway and was killed.[4] God does not limit Himself only to using Christians or spiritually perfect messengers to communicate with us. When you think about it, if that were the case, He wouldn't use any of us as His messengers!

Probably the most likely way God will speak to you through a non-Christian is through those who hold positions of authority in your life. For example, God can speak through your unsaved boss or parent or teacher.

A Canadian Christian businessman told me recently that one of his most trusted advisors is another Canadian businessman who is not a believer. He has been used greatly by the Lord to advise my friend in matters of business. The words he speaks to my friend are the words of God for him.

Discernment is the key to knowing if you are hearing God's voice through a non-Christian's message. The truth is, the same goes for hearing God through a godly person. Either way, we have to trust we will recognize the source. Because the Holy Spirit lives inside of us helping us to recognize God's voice, we usually can discern the advice or message as coming from God or not.

I believe God takes pleasure in surprises and on turning the tables on the unexpected. A friend of ours was facing a time in life when she felt discouraged and stretched thin. Then God unexpectedly spoke to her through an unlikely source—a Barbie story book. Late one night she stopped at a grocery store to pick up some items so she could bake a treat for her elderly grandparents. She grumbled to herself as she stood waiting in line at the checkout. "Do I really need to take time for my elderly grandparents when I have so many other obligations?"

She absentmindedly picked up a children's story book and began reading the story about how Barbie was scheduled to be in a competition but needed to help her elderly neighbor. Subsequently, she arrived late to the competition; however, the judges were so impressed with her that she won the prize anyway.

Our friend heard God speaking through this children's book. "I was convicted and encouraged all at the same time to continue to serve my grandparents and trust God to help take care of everything in my life. With God's strength and priorities I can be a winner, too!"

God loves surprises and wants us to grasp His purpose and message no matter how or through whom He gives it. The Bible encourages us to trust Him to direct us, "Your ears will hear a word behind you, 'This is the way, walk in it,' whenever you turn to the right or to the left."[5] He is faithful, and will direct your path one step at a time. God will get us to the place He wants us to go if we tune our ears to hear His voice without preconceived ideas as to how He will speak in different situations.

Oswald Chambers said, "Jesus rarely comes where we expect Him; He appears where we least expect Him...the only way a servant can remain true to God is to be ready for the Lord's surprise visits. This readiness is expecting Jesus Christ at every turn. This sense of expectation will give our life the attitude of childlike wonder He wants it to have."[6]

Steve, who serves on our international leadership team, has a yellow Labrador Retriever for his family pet. He has shared repeatedly through sermons, teaching illustrations, and even books about how the Lord used his dog, Maggie, to teach him scriptural principles. Unlike Balaam's donkey, Maggie did not literally speak to him, but surprisingly God often gives him a biblical truth through his dog.

Expect the unexpected. At times, God may speak in surprising, dramatic and unpredictable ways!

Hearing God through surprises

Verse to remember: "...Then the Lord opened the donkey's mouth..." (Numbers 22:28).

Apply what you've learned
1. In Numbers 22, a donkey talked for God! Did God ever speak to you in a highly unusual, unexpected way?
2. Did God ever give you an unexpected revelation that you knew was His voice speaking personally to you?
3. Why do you think God likes to surprise us?

Chapter Twentythree

God speaks through
The Unique Way He Made Us

You have your own individual bents, your inherent strengths and preferences, which cause you to have a tendency to hear God's voice in particular ways.

As a young Christian, Julie often compared herself with others and wished she had their particular abilities and personalities. One day while shopping, the Lord nudged Julie toward the wrapping paper section in a little card shop. As she walked toward the bins full of ribbons, she admired all the brightly colored options. The Lord again spoke to her spirit, pointing out that the reason she enjoyed shopping there was the wonderful variety found there. All the wrapping paper and bows were different. The Lord challenged her to recognize He made her the way she was for a reason. She was "wired" for a purpose different than anyone around her. It dawned on her that it was time to quit comparing and start enjoying the person God made her to be!

> **The unique way God made you causes you to tend to hear God in a particular way.**

The scriptures tell us to "Train a child in the way he should go, and when he is old he will not turn from it."[1] The "way he should go" in the Hebrew language means "according to his bent." God wires all of us differently. Individuals have different gifts or "bents" that allow them to hear from God according to the way He has wired them.

We have each been given a purpose from God. If we are to define "purpose," we would say that it is the goal, the function for which your life was conceived, the plan for which you were designed. A microphone, for example, "was born" with everything it needs to receive sounds and transmit them in the form of electrical impulses to an amplifier. It has inside of it each detail, each electronic component, everything it needs to fulfill the task for which it "was born"—to receive sounds and transmit them.

If, instead of a microphone, I took a can opener and tried to use it to receive and transmit sounds, that can opener would be the unhappiest, the most frustrated, and incompetent object ever heard of. Failure, defeat, and unhappiness would take hold of its "emotions." It "was not born" to be a microphone. It was "born" to open cans.

The internal contents of the can opener enable it to fulfill the purpose for which it "was born," which does not include receiving sounds. If I use the can opener to open cans, it will be a "fulfilled" object, because it "found" the place of the purpose for which it exists.

Allow God to speak according to your "bent"

You were born with all the components, all the traits, all the inclinations to fulfill your purpose in life. Everything you need already is inside of you. God conceives His purpose first; then He births it. First of all the prophetic purpose was born in the heart of God. Then, to fulfill it, He called you into being.

When Jeremiah was born, he was already born with all the conditions, with all the heart, with all the inclination, with all the pre-disposition to be a prophet. If Jeremiah had been a musician, he would have been frustrated. If he had been a pastor, he would have been frustrated. If he had been an entrepreneur, or a missionary, he would have been frustrated. He was born to be a prophet of God.

You already have inside of you everything you need to fulfill the high plans of God that will fill your life with harmony and a sense of fulfillment. He is not incoherent. He "manufactured" you. He "knit you together." Your birth was necessary, and, finally, when you were born, you already came into existence, bringing inside of you everything you need to fulfill the purpose of God. Your spiritual genetic code had already been designed by the Author of Life.

The purpose of God came before your own birth. At the moment that God called the prophet Jeremiah, He said, "Before I formed you in the womb I knew you, and before you were born I set you apart; I appointed you as a prophet to the nations."[2] What is God saying here? Is it that He knew you before you were formed? Yes, God knew you even before you existed! It is hard to fathom, but the things of God are higher than ours; they are higher than our simplistic reasoning. Yet it gets even better. The most incredible part of the verse states that even before the birth of the prophet, he had already been appointed as such. Incredible! And since God has a purpose for each of us, and He has wired each of us differently, He is often speaking to us according to the way we are wired.

God speaks through your motivational gift

We have each been given different motivational gifts at birth,

> Just as each of us has one body with many members,
> and these members do not all have the same function,
> so in Christ we who are many form one body, and
> each member belongs to all the others. We have
> different gifts, according to the grace given us. If a
> man's gift is prophesying, let him use it in proportion
> to his faith. If it is serving, let him serve; if it is
> teaching, let him teach; if it is encouraging, let him
> encourage; if it is contributing to the needs of others,
> let him give generously; if it is leadership, let him

govern diligently; if it is showing mercy, let him do it cheerfully.[3]

We each have different motivations in life, and the Lord often speaks to us through our personal motivation. For instance, if you have a motivational gift of giving, the Lord will probably speak to you about giving more than the average person, because you just love to give.

As a high school student, Sarah, who now oversees our church's publication department, began to realize she was good at visual art. As her walk with God deepened, she recognized God had given her these abilities, and He probably wanted her to use the gifts she had been given. She began choosing classes that helped her develop those gifts. Sarah went on to study graphic design and today loves her job as a graphic artist.

God wants us to enjoy what we are doing. If you cannot hold a tune, the Lord is not calling you to be a worship leader. That would waste your time as well as God's true call on your life because He has not wired you for musical endeavors. Some people think that if the Lord speaks to them to do something, it will be something that they hate doing. This could not be farther from the truth! God wired you perfectly to speak to you and fulfill His purpose through you.

Be who God made you to be!

You should ask yourself, "What burns in the depths of my spirit? What desire is in there? Am I hungry to learn more, to serve the kingdom, to be a business owner, to be a pastor, a missionary, a prophet, an intercessor, an entrepreneur or used in the ministry of helping others?" A great evidence that shows these thoughts are not mere daydreams of your mind is to ask, "Is my heart overflowing with joy and faith when I think about these things?" There is a purpose of God to be fulfilled in your life. God often answers these questions through our natural gifts and abilities. He leads us to our purpose through the natural skills and unique talents He bestows upon us.

Hearing God

God-given gifts are the skills a person easily performs without formal training. For example, many songwriters just sit down and write the music they hear in their heads. Some people are great at organizing, while others are natural counselors. We derive great pleasure from doing what we are naturally good at doing. God speaks to us through these natural gifts. These natural gifts can obviously be honed and developed with formal training.

If you aren't sure of your purpose in life, just do what you are good at doing, and then watch God confirm you by blessing your endeavors. Do not spend your life trying to do what you are not gifted to do. I tried to minister to children in a Sunday School class, but soon realized it was not my gift. When we started our new church, I preached one Sunday and ministered to the children in Sunday School the next. Those poor kids put up with me every other week! Teaching in the children's ministry just was not my gift.

I also had a tendency to get bogged down by trying to be a counselor, because it was not how God wired me. Yet I have traveled to dozens of nations, find myself ministering in a different city nearly every weekend and fly well over 100,000 miles each year. I have spent many nights sleeping on airplane seats because I need to immediately go to a meeting or radio station to speak when I land, and believe it or not, this energizes me. I come home from a long trip, traveling to the other side of the world, and seldom experience jet lag. I have become comfortable with how God has made me and no longer try to be someone else. It has been so freeing to me. How has the Lord wired you? Stop trying to be someone you are not.

As a young woman, Elizabeth recognized that she was wired to lead. As she matured in her Christian life, she began to utilize her gifting as a leader who truly enjoyed planning larger events. She had a memory that could sort through and remember many details, but the gift seemed so masculine to her. She recalls, "I had to make a choice. Was I going to use the gifts God gave me to build up the body of Christ or hide them? I decided to trust God to become the woman of God He wanted me to be, not the person I thought I should be." This revelation empowered her to realize her potential to hear from God the way He had wired her.

Genesis 4:20-22 tells us that Jabal was the father of those who raised cattle. His brother Jubal was the father of all the musicians who played the lyre and pipe. His half-brother Tubal-Cain forged instruments made of bronze and iron. They were all different with specific gifts from the Lord.

God keeps our world in balance by giving each of us natural talents and pleasure in doing what needs to be done for the good of everyone around us. Aren't you glad everyone is not like you? All kinds of gifts and abilities are needed to get God's job done. God speaks to us through our natural talents and abilities.

When you get in touch with how God has wired you, it will be a pleasure and not a burden to your life. God will not violate your likes and dislikes. He will work in line with what you like to do. We need to understand that, from the spiritual point of view, our heart desires and leans toward things that, since eternity, God has already brought into line for us to be involved in.

Influenced by emotion rather than your design

At times we can be influenced by emotional messages of the soul that make us have a natural zeal in the things of God. In some countries it is common for people to be awakened to missionary service, for instance, as a result of hearing speakers at conferences. Because of the great needs in the mission field, these sincere Christians think they will do a great service to God, thrusting themselves into the field to meet this challenge.

What a gross mistake. How common it is to see missionaries that are defeated, frustrated and filled with bitterness. Their families are sometimes disillusioned. What a tragedy! God has not called them, but even so they have gone. If in actuality the dream has come from God, it will be a wonderful experience—fulfilling, satisfactory, and filled with excitement, even though there might be suffering, challenges and a lot of work. In spite of some occasional struggles or failures, the greatest conviction will be the constant and confirming direction of the Holy Spirit, who generated this dream and call.

God has made you uniquely; you are one of a kind. He will speak to you and lead you according to the way He has shaped you for His service. Many times, when I have asked God what He wanted me to do in a specific situation, He has spoken to my heart, "Do what you want to do." He gives us more and more liberty as we grow spiritually into a state of maturity.

I often think of my own children. When they were young and inexperienced, my wife and I made all of their decisions for them; but as they got older and more mature, we let them do more of what they wanted to do according to how the Lord made them.

Maybe you are trying to hear from God about your life when in actuality, He is speaking to you already through the way He has made you. Trust those inner leadings and nudges that come from the way God wired you.

Hearing God through the unique way He made us

Verse to remember "Train a child in the way he should go [according to his bent], and when he is old he will not turn from it" (Proverbs 22:6).

Apply what you've learned
1. What are your particular strengths and preferences causing you to hear God most often in a certain way?
2. How do you nurture the natural gifts that God gives?
3. What burns in the depths of your spirit? Does God speak to you through this desire?

God speaks through
Signs

Sometimes we just need to know if we are on the right track, so we ask the Lord to confirm His will by giving us a sign.

A few years ago Florida motorists received some tongue-in-cheek messages "signed" by God in the form of a billboard campaign. Large signs were emblazoned with short messages from God saying things like, "We need to talk."—God.

Other signs said,

"I can think of ten things that are carved in stone."

"I don't question *your* existence."

"Will the road you're on get you to my place?"

"Keep taking my name in vain and I'll make rush hour longer."

"Have you read my #1 best seller? There will be a test."

These signs endeavored to get people to reconsider that God still speaks today and

God sometimes allows you to ask for a sign to confirm that He is speaking.

has timeless truth to offer mankind. I don't know if God actually spoke to anyone's need with these roadside signs, but I'd like to think that He did. I believe God loves to grab our attention and speak to us in unexpected ways.

Did you ever lack direction for your life and just didn't know what to do, so you picked up your Bible, flipped it open and pointed at a verse? This is an example of attempting to hear God's voice by asking for a special message or sign from Him.

Or, if we are having trouble hearing from God, we may attempt to put God to the test, so to speak, to make sure that God is speaking to us. This kind of attempt to hear God's voice by asking for a specific sign is often called "laying out a fleece." We get this term from Gideon's experience in the Bible.

In Judges we read the story about Gideon desiring a sign and laying out a fleece before the Lord for confirmation and direction. Gideon wanted to be doubly sure that what God said was really what God wanted him to do. Gideon said to God,

> "If you will save Israel by my hand as you have promised—look, I will place a wool fleece on the threshing floor. If there is dew only on the fleece and all the ground is dry, then I will know that you will save Israel by my hand, as you said." And that is what happened. Gideon rose early the next day; he squeezed the fleece and wrung out the dew—a bowlful of water. Then Gideon said to God, "Do not be angry with me. Let me make just one more request. Allow me one more test with the fleece. This time make the fleece dry and the ground covered with dew." That night God did so. Only the fleece was dry; all the ground was covered with dew.[1]

Notice that Gideon still wasn't sure about the first sign and asked the Lord to do the reverse of the sign to confirm it. He wanted to be sure this was really God speaking to him. I believe this shows that if we resort to fleeces, we should receive confirmation in other ways to be sure we are receiving clear direction from the Lord.

Some other signs God used in the past to speak

Without a doubt, God used signs to speak dramatically throughout the history of mankind. In Genesis, He sent a well-known sign that took the form of a rainbow. This sign was a promise of God's covenant between Himself and every living creature on earth. God said,

> "This is the sign of the covenant I am making between me and you and every living creature with you, a covenant for all generations to come: I have set my rainbow in the clouds, and it will be the sign of the covenant between me and the earth. Whenever I bring clouds over the earth and the rainbow appears in the clouds, I will remember my covenant between me and you and all living creatures of every kind."[2]

On another occasion, God sent a supernatural sign that stopped time. The sun stood still for a day so the Israelites could fight and win a battle. Only God could manage such a feat, causing the Israelites to recognize that God was on their side.

> On the day the Lord gave the Amorites over to Israel, Joshua said to the Lord in the presence of Israel: "O sun, stand still over Gibeon, O moon, over the Valley of Aijalon." So the sun stood still, and the moon stopped, till the nation avenged itself on its enemies...There has never been a day like it before or since, a day when the Lord listened to a man. Surely the Lord was fighting for Israel![3]

Cautions in hearing God through signs

We should use caution and not become dependent on these kinds of signs to hear from God, because they are rather unusual ways to confirm His will. Additionally, we should probably not depend on a sign to be the sole factor in making a decision; however, it is clear that the Lord will sometimes honor and answer our request for a sign.

Someone once said that our goal should "not be to improve our testing of God's will, but to improve our relationship with God." God really wants a relationship with you and me that is strong enough so we can understand what He is saying without "testing" Him. We can become spiritually lazy in looking for signs, when we should be learning to listen to and discern God's voice. If we learn to hear His Spirit's voice, we will not need to set up a complicated test to see if it is really Him.

There are times that God does allow Himself to be tested. I believe He understands there are times when we need and desire proof. God recognized this need in Gideon. He knew that in order for Gideon to overcome his fear he needed proof so that he could go to the next level. And God answered Gideon twice with a supernatural intrusion into the laws of nature!

The care we have to take in using "fleeces" is that they may consist of varying circumstances that could just as easily take place without any input from God at all! We may say to ourselves, "If this light turns green before I reach the intersection...or if a certain song comes on the radio, God is speaking this or that to me." We really should accompany this kind of a fleece by scriptural confirmation and further guidance through prayer. One young man once told me he was basing his decision about marrying a certain young woman on whether or not the next traffic light turned green or red. In my opinion, this is not seeking a sign, it is utter foolishness!

Nevertheless, sometimes it is appropriate to ask for a sign— and God will answer. God responded to Gideon's lack of faith because He knew Gideon's heart wanted to obey. If the Lord knows we want to obey, there are times He will strengthen our faith by giving us a sign.

Seeking a sign is certainly a valid way to ask God to speak to us in certain instances, but it should not be used exclusively for hearing from God. God does not always give us the solution to our dilemmas with instant answers, nor should we require Him to. God primarily wants a relationship with us. He invites us to get to know Him and have a close relationship with Him, so we will recognize His voice in the many, many different ways He speaks.

Hearing God through signs

Verse to remember "...I will place a wool fleece on the threshing floor. If there is dew only on the fleece and all the ground is dry, then I will know that you will save Israel by my hand, as you said" (Judges 6:37).

Apply what you've learned
1. For what reason might this not be the most preferred way to hear from God?
2. How can it be "spiritually lazy" to ask for a sign?
3. Has God ever spoken to you through a sign? Explain.

God speaks through
Practicing His Presence

God is never away from you. He is continually present in your life.

As a Christian, your body is the temple of the Holy Spirit and God takes up permanent residence there. God wants you to live daily in His presence. He longs for you to open your spiritual ears to hear Him speak as you walk through your daily life. How is it possible to live minute by minute in the presence of God?

When you are learning a new language, at first you are insecure and uncertain; however, as you practice, you become more secure and learn the new language's distinguishing sounds. Living minute by minute in the presence of God takes practice. It involves learning to open your spiritual ears.

When he realized that he could continually be in the presence of God, Max Lucado recalls how it revolutionized his life:

> For years I viewed God as a compassionate CEO and my role as a loyal sales representative. He had His office, and I had my territory. I could contact Him as much as I wanted. He was always a phone or fax away. He encouraged me, rallied behind

Practicing His presence means keeping your spiritual ears open, even in the routine of daily life.

me, and supported me, but He didn't go with me. At least I didn't think He did. Then I read 2 Corinthians 6:1: "We are God's fellow workers."

Fellow workers? Colaborers? God and I work together? Imagine the paradigm shift this truth creates. Rather than report to God, we work with God. Rather than check in with Him and then leave, we check in with Him and then follow. We are always in the presence of God. We never leave church. There is never a nonsacred moment! His presence never diminishes. Our awareness of His presence may falter, but the reality of His presence never changes.[1]

The reality of His presence in daily life

The Lord says, "Be still, and know that I am God."[2] God wants us to experience His presence and continually maintain a God-consciousness. Daily, we can enjoy unceasing communion with God, finding in Him all that we need all of the time.

Since "being still" is a presence of mind—a state of rest in the Lord, it does not necessarily mean you have to find a solitary place and shut everything else out, although there are times this is necessary. A mother of young children does not have the option of having extended times of solitude, but it is possible to experience God's presence in the daily routine of changing dirty diapers and carpooling the kids to soccer practice.

I believe that practicing the presence of God can take place in the midst of your routine as you learn to tune your spirit to loving the Lord with your whole heart, soul and mind. When you want to please God in your thoughts, deeds and words, your will becomes united with God's will. This affects your attitude as you love God with no other motive than to love Him and listen for His voice.

Brother Lawrence, a monk from the seventeenth century, known for his book *The Practice of the Presence of God,* said, "We must know before we can love. In order to know God, we must often think of Him. And when we come to love Him, we shall then also think of Him often, for our heart will be with our treasure." Brother Lawrence described this continuous practice of the presence of God as a "quiet, familiar conversation with Him."[3]

> The most effective way Brother Lawrence had for communicating with God was to simply do his ordinary work. He did this obediently, out of a pure love of God, purifying it as much as was humanly possible. He believed it was a serious mistake to think of our prayer time as being different from any other. He said, "I turn my little omelet in the pan for the love of God."[4]

Learn to listen intentionally

Walking in the loving presence of God daily and making each day one continuous prayer can be compared to the biblical challenge to "pray without ceasing."[5] But how is it possible to fellowship with God continually? Can it become as natural as breathing? I believe it can. But we must learn to listen.

Bible teacher Joyce Meyer told her husband one day that they needed to talk more. It seemed to Joyce that he never wanted to just spend time sitting and talking. Her husband responded by saying, "Joyce, we don't talk; *you* talk and I listen."

Joyce confirms, "He was right, and I needed to change if I expected him to want to fellowship with me. I also discovered I was doing the same thing with God; I talked and expected God to listen. I complained that I never heard from God, but the truth is I never listened."[6]

This is a good lesson for all of us. For most, listening is an ability that must be developed by practice. If you are a born talker, you never had to work hard at making conversation; but you may have had to make an effort to listen intentionally.

My wife LaVerne who has learned over the years the importance of communing with God and having a real love relationship with our Father in heaven describes it like this:

> We as a church are engaged to Jesus, the bridegroom who is coming back for us—the bride. What do engaged couples do to have an effective relationship? They spend time together, not just talking, but listening to each other's heart, sharing each other's dreams. As they listen and talk together, they understand each other. If they just talk and do not listen, they have an ineffective relationship. So it is in our relationship with Jesus. It is Jesus' desire that we listen to Him and commune with Him. We need to see that we are engaged to Him and the Word of God needs to be powerful in our lives.
>
> When the Word of God is in us, we understand and know who God is. We understand that He wants to speak to us. The Word of God is spirit and life within us. As we drive down the road, as we wash dishes, as we sit at our desk, we are aware of His presence and are willing to listen to that "still, small voice" based on the Word of God, because the Word of God is in us. God desires to speak to us all day long. It is up to us to listen to Him.

Growing and hearing go hand-in-hand

According to Hebrews 5:11-14, sometimes our hearing becomes dulled because we are not listening to or obeying the truth we already know. Paul expressed his disappointment with the Hebrew Christians because they had not grown up spiritually and learned to hear and obey God's voice.

> ...though by this time you ought to be teachers, you need someone to teach you the elementary truths of

God's word all over again. You need milk, not solid food! Anyone who lives on milk, being still an infant, is not acquainted with the teaching about righteousness. But solid food is for the mature, who by constant use have trained themselves to distinguish good from evil.

Babies are not ready for solid food They need to grow first. As spiritual babies grow and mature, they eventually learn to hear and obey God's voice. The Lord does not reveal everything to baby Christians at once; He explains things to them as they are able to understand. If they obey the truth they have, the Lord will be able to reveal new truths He wants them to know.

God will tell us the way to go, but then we have to do the walking, one step of obedience at a time. The Bible says, "The steps of a good man are ordered by the Lord, And He delights in his way. Though he fall, he shall not be utterly cast down; For the Lord upholds him with His hand."[7] Start right where you are and learn to enjoy practicing His presence in simple faith.

It is okay to make mistakes. Don't be discouraged. By faith, get up and start again. Life is like an American football game. Every time there is a play, the quarterback gets his team into a huddle and they come up with a new play: it is all part of a larger game plan. God gathers us into His huddle and gives us a new plan for the next steps in our game of life.

Jesus gave His life for us on the cross two thousand years ago. He paid the price for us to experience a loving relationship with our heavenly Father. Practicing His presence in our lives each day is about nurturing a love-filled relationship with Him that lasts forever!

Hearing God
through practicing His presence

Verse to remember: "Enoch walked with God..." (Genesis 5:24).

Apply what you've learned

1. How can you make each day one continuous prayer?
2. How will practicing God's presence as described in this chapter help you to hear God's voice?
3. What are some practical ways you plan to practice God's presence in your daily routine of life?

Chapter Twentysix

God speaks through
His Silence

There are times it seems the Lord is nowhere to be found.

Our prayers feel like they are hitting the ceiling and bouncing back. We feel far from God—like we have entirely lost our way. Every Christian goes through these "dark nights of the soul" in our walk with the Lord when He is silent.

You are not alone. Jesus understands how you feel. He cried out in anguish, "Father, why have you forsaken me?" Even Jesus knew His Father's silence.

Sometimes we fail to hear from God because we are not paying attention, but what about those times when we really are listening but somehow we can no longer sense Him speaking? At times God's reasons for being silent are to get our attention so we can receive clear spiritual direction that

God's silence may occur when He is poised to do His deepest work in our lives.

will go to the core of our being. His silence may occur when He is poised to do His deepest work in our lives.

His silence is a reminder of how desperately we need Him

We should not fear God's silence because it really is a reminder that we need Him so desperately. When He is silent and

God Speaks Through His Silence 177

life seems dark, it often motivates us to place our full trust in God. We pay more attention when we are lost in the woods! God may be building our character so we can be more effective in His kingdom. In the darkness of God's silence, we are reminded of what we are missing.

Bob Mumford once said, "I do not trust anyone unless he walks with a limp." I agree with him. He was referring to Jacob, who during a time of great trial in his life, wrestled with God, demanding His blessing. He was touched in his thigh and did in fact receive the Lord's blessing. But from that day on, he walked with a limp. When God lovingly deals with us in the difficult times, we walk with a spiritual limp the rest of our lives. This is the stuff of which true spiritual men and women of God are made.

Peter was a disciple who "walked with a limp." Zealous and brash, he denied Jesus, but later experienced God's complete acceptance, forgiveness and restoration and became a true father in the faith.

Refuse to quit during God's "silent test"

The Bible is filled with examples of those who started with an exciting experience of hearing from the Lord, refused to quit when God was silent, and consequently experienced great fruitfulness because they kept their confidence and trust in the Lord. The story of Joseph in the Old Testament is one of the best. After having a dream that his brothers would bow down to him, he encountered trial after trial. Joseph was sold as a slave by his brothers, lied about by his employer's wife, imprisoned while innocent, forgotten in prison, only to become second in command of all of Egypt overnight! Although it must have felt to him that God had left him in prison to die, he entered the stage of great fruitfulness as he refused to give up during the difficult seasons of his life.

God used this stage of testing in Joseph's life to examine his character. God gave him an attitude check, and he passed the test. He could then be a blessing to his brothers who had severely mistreated him in the past. Many quit during the test period, when the Lord seems to stop speaking, and never experience the stage of fruitfulness the Lord has planned for them.

The Lord is much more concerned about what He is doing in you than about you reaching your goals. He wants you to depend on Him and on His power in the here and now. Oswald Chambers once said, "If I can stay calm, faithful, and unconfused while in the middle of the turmoil of life, the goal of the purpose of God is being accomplished in me. God is not working toward a particular finish—His purpose is the process itself."[1] God's silence will reveal our true attitudes toward God by showing us what is really in our hearts and then giving us the opportunity to fully trust in His power as we persevere.

Is God's silence one of judgment?

While it is true that God sometimes is silent due to no fault of our own because He is simply developing within us a depth of character and a deeper trust in Him, at other times He is silent due to disobedience in our lives. King David once said, "If I had not confessed the sin in my heart, my Lord would not have listened."[2] Sin alienates us from God, and creates a barrier to hearing from Him. In times like these, God's silences may be an act of judgment.

In the days of Samuel the prophet, the priests were ungodly men, and the Bible says "the word of the Lord was rare."[3] God refused to speak because these rebellious priests misrepresented God to the people. God's silence was a stamp of disapproval on the behavior of the priests. Because they didn't hear God's voice for a period of time, the people became hungry to hear it again. God's silence paved the way for Samuel to be heard as God's spokesman.

If we cannot hear God's voice because God is chastising us with His silence, we must examine ourselves to see what is hindering us from hearing.

Go back to where we last heard God's voice

How do we discover what it is that God wants to show us? There is a story in the Old Testament that gives us some insight. A man was cutting down a tree by the river when his iron ax head fell into the water. An ax head was a very expensive tool, and the man desperately wanted to retrieve it because it was borrowed. He went to Elisha, a man of God, for help. Elisha asked where he had last seen it fall, threw a stick in the water, and it miraculously floated to the surface![4] At the same place that it was lost, the ax head reappeared!

We can learn an important lesson from this. Whenever we have problems with finding direction in our lives, it is often helpful to go back to where we were certain we last heard the voice of the Lord clearly. If we do not go back, we may continue to flounder.

I used to feel compelled to try to find shortcuts whenever I drove somewhere. It was a source of tension between LaVerne and me because I usually got lost! To backtrack over and over again was embarrassing! More often than not, I needed to go back to the last road I was familiar with before I could find the way.

If we find ourselves in a spiritual wasteland and wandering aimlessly, it is not the end of the world. The Bible says that the Lord is able to "restore...the years that the swarming locust has eaten."[5] God offers hope if we are experiencing His silence because of sin in our lives. If we have lost our spiritual way, the Bible says we must, "Remember the height from which you have fallen! Repent and do the things you did at first...."[6] Repentance takes us back to the place where we last heard from God. Restoration comes as the Lord gives us a new start.

A few years ago, LaVerne and I bought a time share near Orlando, Florida. Although there is nothing wrong with purchasing a time share, we knew immediately we had made a mistake. Instead of following our personal policy of taking time to pray and not make a quick decision, we bought it impulsively and under pressure from the sales pitch. We went off-track from what we knew was the Lord's best for us.

We quickly repented for not following our personal value of waiting and praying, and after asking the Lord to restore our mistake, I felt He said that He would redeem it for us in two years. And that is exactly what happened. Two years later we were able to sell it.

God's silence teaches us to wait on Him

As mentioned before, God's silence is not always linked to sin in our lives. Sometimes, He is just teaching us to wait on Him and trust in His faithfulness. In 1992, I began to question whether or not I was called to church leadership. Anything else looked much better than to continue on in a leadership role; however, I remembered the initial call when God called me to start a new church in 1980. This was the place the ax head had fallen for me, and I was convinced the Lord had spoken to me and given me a mandate to start the church. Knowing this gave me the confidence to continue on even though it seemed like He wasn't there. I knew He had not yet completed the work He had begun. He was doing a much deeper work in my life, teaching me to wait and trust only in Him, not on my own strengths or abilities.

When God is silent, we must choose to trust His silence, quiet ourselves and wait on Him. Listen to Isaiah's words about God waiting for us to be silent:

> In returning and *rest* you shall be saved; in *quietness* and in trust shall be your strength...the Lord *waits* to be gracious to you...blessed are all those who *wait* for him.[7]

Remember, roots grow deep into the earth during times of drought to find water to give the tree a better foundation. Times of God's silence prepare us for future storms.

God's silence of love

In addition to God's silence of waiting, He also speaks to us in His silence of love. Zephaniah, the prophet, describes this silence of love: "He will be quiet in His love."[8] Writer Paul Thigpen says that the deepest sorrows and the highest joys are best shared in silence:

> I remember two quiet, wordless moments that reflected this truth in my own life. One took place when I stood silently by my father's casket at his funeral. The other came when I stood watching my firstborn child, only a few moments old, and wept silently over the miracle that had made me a father.[9]

God is silent because words will distract from the love and care God is conveying to us in His quietness.

If you are going through a time in your life where God seems distant, pray for wisdom to interpret the silences. Whether He is silent to test you, judge you or quiet you in His love, He always intends that you put your trust in Him so He can do a deep work in you. You can trust Him.

When God is silent, it doesn't mean that He is absent. King David, on more than one occasion, felt abandoned by God. Yet despite the silence, David knew he was never out of God's sight. "Where can I go from your Spirit: Where can I flee from your presence?...If I settle on the far side of the sea, even there your hand will guide me, your right hand will hold me fast...."[10]

God promises never to leave us or forsake us.[11] His silence should be our cue to hunger and thirst after Him even more. His silence is a reminder of what we are missing. Painful dry spells drive us closer to Him. It has been well said, "Never forget in the dark what you have learned in the light."

Hearing God through His silence

Verse to remember "Where can I go from your Spirit? Where can I flee from your presence? If I go up to the heavens, you are there; if I make my bed in the depths, you are there" (Psalm 139:7-8).

Apply what you've learned
1. The old song says that "silence is golden." Why does silence from God never feel that way?
2. Have I obeyed the last thing the Lord asked me to do?
3. Most of us thrive on some type of noise around us (TV, CD player, children playing). Is there something that we are afraid of?
4. Describe any times you heard God's "silence of waiting" or "silence of love."

Chapter Twentyseven

God speaks through
Partial Revelation

The Bible tells us we all "know in part...."[1] *God rarely gives one person the entire perspective.*

It is not a weakness in our relationship with the Lord when we only have a piece of the puzzle. When the Lord speaks to us everything is seldom crystal-clear. We often miss some of the details, and we sometimes make assumptions of what we believe the Lord has spoken.

Sometimes God speaks to our spirit, but our soul (mind, will and emotions) gets entangled with our inner voice. We get a message that is not completely from the Lord. I mentioned earlier in this book, that if you have ever taken a drink out of a garden hose you will taste both the water and the hose. This analogy applies to hearing from the Lord. Sometimes what we hear is partially the Lord and is at the same time partially us.

> **God partially reveals Himself because He wants you to step out in faith.**

Step out in faith

People often ask me, "How do I find the destiny the Lord has called me to? I just do not have a complete picture of what God is saying." Some people spend many years waiting to hear a voice from heaven or wait until they receive supernatural direction. Many never receive it.

I believe we must step out in faith, and God will lead us from there. It is hard to steer a car that is not moving. You may need to be moving if you want God to show you which way to go. The Lord tells us, "A man's mind plans his way, but the Lord directs his steps and makes them sure."[2] He leads one step at a time; and if you take one step forward, and it's the wrong way, He will let you know before you go too far. Step out in faith and find out which doors God will open for you and which ones He will close.

Baby steps of faith

If you've ever seen the movie, "What About Bob?" you will remember that a therapy patient, who fears everything, is initially advised by his therapist to take "baby steps" so he can learn to function normally. The comical story takes us through the many antics of Bob as he learns to take those first steps.

This advice of taking "baby steps" is well advised. Taking small, slow steps at first will prevent us from falling so hard if we are wrong! We can stick our toes in the water to test the water, so to speak. Take one small step of faith. If God opens the door, then take another step. If He closes the door, then back off. Try another direction, or wait a while; but always keep praying and then step out again.

Even the parents of Jesus had to make some adjustments in their direction until they had it right. An angel of the Lord appeared to Joseph in a dream and told him to take baby Jesus back to Israel. So Joseph headed in that direction, but on the way was frightened to hear that the new king was Herod's son who also wanted to kill Jesus. Then in another dream Joseph was warned not to go to Judea, so they went to Galilee instead, and lived in Nazareth.[3] Joseph and Mary were not sure what steps they should take, but they took one step at a time. The Lord knows that He could overwhelm us by revealing the whole plan at once. We might be frightened and not take the first step. Consequently, He leads us just one step at a time so we can handle it.

God doesn't push us out into the cold with only a map in our hands. He leads us by providing His Holy Spirit to guide us. He wants us to keep our eyes on Him, and then to follow alongside Him one step at a time.

God speaks with incremental guidance

Paul, the apostle, as intimate as He was with God, did not always hear the entire message from the Lord all at one time. He had to take one step at a time. On one missionary journey, he and his companions were making their way toward Ephesus, but God stopped them. Then he started northward into Bithynia, and again God stopped him. Then he turned northwest, and came to Troas. Finally, Paul had a dream and saw a man pleading with him to come to Macedonia which was where God wanted him. Many came to Christ there.[4] This is an example of incremental guidance where Paul heard God's voice in part, and step by step he discovered the way God wanted him to go.

Abraham is another example of someone who trusted God to lead him one step at a time. His story in Genesis 12:1 describes the start of his faith journey: "Now the Lord said to Abram, 'Go for yourself away from your country, from your relatives and your father's house, to the land that I will show you.'" God gave Abraham step one. He implied that he wasn't getting step two or three until he had accomplished step one. This sounds like common sense, but it is so true: God usually gives us His direction one step at a time.

Many people run into a problem here. They refuse to take step one until they think they understand the next steps. If we know all the steps ahead of time, there is no need for faith. Understanding this truth that His will is usually revealed to us one step at a time will build our confidence to do what we already know to do—step out. After we take the first few steps, our faith will really begin to grow.

Hearing God

At times, we are stretched in faith as we step out to do things that we do not have any experience at or are not comfortable doing at first. I am convinced that no one is instantly a spiritual giant who takes great steps of faith in the beginning. Faith grows and develops through experience.

Trust is so important when we take those "faith steps." Did you ever ask God to supply a financial need and God came through, but only at the last minute? I think the Lord sometimes gives us what we need at the very last moment because faith grows by stretching!

Obeying God even when it doesn't make sense

Faith is the bottom line when it comes to learning to hear the voice of the Lord. The Bible says, "Now faith is being sure of what we hope for and certain of what we do not see."[5] A weatherman uses radar and satellite to predict a storm coming. He is sure the storm is coming, but he cannot prove it because it has not yet physically arrived. When the storm comes it is no longer *faith*, but *reality*. Once we have a manifestation of what we desire in our circumstance, we no longer need faith in that area. But until we hear God's voice, we need faith!

Soldiers in military training are sometimes required to do things that don't make sense. Military boot camp is extremely difficult. It is designed to take the recruit to his limit. If under extreme physical and mental pressure he does not fall apart, he may qualify for military service. If not, he will be sent home never seeing or experiencing military life. Why?

The new recruits must learn to obey quickly without questioning their superiors. If they are on the front lines of battle, and their leaders give them a command, they could get killed if they turn to ask, "Why?" In the same way, God wants us to learn to trust Him and just obey, even if it does not always make complete sense to us.

The Bible says that the natural man does not understand the spiritual man.[6] This means that our reasoning mind often does not understand our spiritual mind which is "the mind of Christ."[7] The Holy Spirit reveals things to us when we are ready to handle them. If He revealed everything that's wrong with us at once, we would be crushed.

We learn, through maturing in Christ, that if our heart is right, and we trust and obey the Lord when He speaks, God will honor our steps of obedience. We may make mistakes but God will take our mistakes and turn them around for good. The fact that everything works toward our good does not mean it will always feel good or that we will enjoy the process. His Word says that He makes "all things work together for good to those who love God, to those called according to His purpose,"[8] and we can trust His Word.

After serving the Lord for many years, I am totally convinced that it is more difficult to get out of His will than we often think. If we do stray off course, He will reach out in love and nudge us back on track.

God answers despite our partial hearing

Jo was awakened very early one Saturday morning and sensed God was calling her to prayer. She did not know exactly who or what to pray for, so she started to pray for family and friends.

Without a strong sense of direction, she ended her prayer time by praying for protection for everyone. She didn't want to leave anyone out!

When she discovered that her roommate's boyfriend was in a plane crash later that morning, she recalled having prayed for protection for everyone without knowing why. Now she knew! There was no loss of life in the plane crash. Partially hearing from God on Jo's part did not prohibit God from moving miraculously.

Relax, don't strive

It is easier than we think it is to hear the voice of the Lord. We really have to stop trying so hard; in fact, God's Word says, "The servant of the Lord must not strive."[9]

Relax and enjoy your relationship with the Lord. Remember, His sheep hear His voice. He is our shepherd and when we begin to get off track, He reaches out His staff and guides us back on the right track. The key is for us to stay submissive to His will and voice. I have found that if what I am sensing is from God, it stays with me for a period of time.

We certainly need to discern the Lord's voice carefully, but let's not over-spiritualize hearing from God. If God has something to say to us, don't worry, He knows how to get His point across. It is our responsibility to listen with expectancy and test what we hear.

It appears that the "normal" method of operations between David and God was for David to do what was in his heart, and God promised He would be with him. This is reflected in Psalm 37:4, "Delight yourself also in the Lord, and He will give you the desires and secret petitions of your heart."

This works two ways: first, He gives us what we long for; but secondly, He also places a longing in our hearts for things He wants us to have. David, however, never assumed that God's direction for one day would be the same the next day. He listened for the Lord's instructions for each battle he fought.[10]

Philippians 2:13 says it similarly, "For it is God who works in you to will and to act according to his good purpose." God places desires within us to lead us in the way He wants us to go.

God is at work in our lives, teaching us to listen and then obey the voice of the Lord. Most Christians never have a face-to-face encounter with Jesus as Paul did on his way to Damascus. Even Paul didn't always experience the heavens opening up or angels appearing every time God spoke to him. We are led by His Spirit speaking to our spirits every day of our lives.

Let's continue to listen to the Lord, recognize that He speaks to us because of His wonderful grace, all the while realizing that we are only hearing a part of the whole message. He may want to speak more to us, and He may want to use another method to speak. This keeps us dependent on our growing relationship with Him.

Hearing God through partial revelation

Verse to remember "For we know in part..." (1 Corinthians 13:9).

Apply what you've learned
1. How do we tend to over-spiritualize or make it too difficult in hearing from God?
2. Why do you think God often gives us only a piece of the puzzle?
3. What part does faith play in hearing from God?
4. Tell of a time you heard "in part" from God, stepped out in faith, and the rest came.

PART III

Keys to Hearing From God

Chapter Twentyeight

Beware the Enemy's Schemes

The enemy of your soul does not want you to hear from the Lord!
The devil will try to discourage you and place traps in your path to trip you up as you endeavor to listen to the Lord. You are in warfare against the powers of darkness. Let's take a look at some of the traps for you to be aware of as you travel on your journey of listening to the voice of God.

Counterfeits of the Holy Spirit's work

The Bible says that in the last days many false prophets will rise up and tell people what their ears want to hear. People will gravitate toward teachers who tell them something pleasing and gratifying. To suit their own desires, they will turn away from hearing the truth and will wander off into listening to myths and man-made fictions.[1]

Today we can turn on our television and find shows that feature psychics who claim to be connecting in the spiritual realm with departed loved ones. These mediums communicate with "familiar" spirits who tell half-truths about the past and fabricate the future.

God's Word clearly tells us, "Turn not to those [mediums] who have familiar spirits or to wizards; do not seek them out to be defiled by them. I am the Lord your God."[2] The seriousness of entertaining familiar spirits (a type of evil spirit) is plainly set forth in God's Word. Spiritualism, witchcraft, and divination are all forbidden in the Word of God.

Yet some Christians still read horoscopes and consult psychics, and then they wonder why they don't have peace in their lives. They are walking in deception.

Our faith must be in God alone. Believers in Jesus Christ do not depend on luck or the predictions of a psychic, they depend on the grace of God and on His ability to bless them.

A young woman in a remote village in the interior of the nation of Suriname desired freedom from "harassing spirits." As her church leaders prayed, it was discerned that there was something demonic about a gold charm on her necklace. This precious woman was unwilling to renounce the charm, and her deliverance was unsuccessful. By those persons with experience in this type of prayer, it was concluded that what seemed like an innocent good luck charm was actually permission for the enemy to harass her soul.

The enemy will scheme in any way to keep you from hearing from God and will create a counterfeit. Did you ever get one of those "Christian" chain emails with inspirational stories that ask you to pass it along to 10 people you care about in 48 hours if you really love God? These emails are little different from those that predict bad luck if they are not forwarded. Forwarding an email will not prove your love for God.

By deceiving us with superstitions motivated by guilt, Satan tries to counterfeit God's true voice in our lives. We have to counter these schemes with the Word of God that clearly says the Holy Spirit dwells inside of each one of us and will lead us individually. Entrusting ourselves into the hands of our loving Father will help us develop an ability to hear and be led by His Spirit. We must tune our ears to hear and trust the wisdom God has deposited in our own heart as we discern His voice.

Noise interference

One of the devil's schemes is to pollute your mind with noise and action. We live in a fast-paced society, with multi-tasking a commonplace feat. I can drive a car, talk on my cell phone, drink coffee, and listen to my favorite CD, all at the same time. At my desk, I can instant message a friend in Austria, email a co-worker, buy an item on E-Bay and balance my checkbook, all within a few seconds.

I believe the devil strives to increase the noise in our lives, and it often prevents us from hearing God. Too often we miss God's voice because of being distracted. C.S. Lewis states that for a Christian the "first job of the day is to shove back the wishes and hopes for the day that rush at you like wild animals. Listen for that other voice...."[3]

Idols in our hearts

God's voice will be distorted if you place something or someone ahead of Him.[4] The prophet Ezekiel tells how the elders of Israel came to him to get information about the future, but God saw their idolatrous hearts and would not give them an answer.[5]

If you come to God asking Him for something that you have not submitted to Him inwardly, it becomes an idol in your heart. If you fix your gaze on a desire in your heart instead of on Jesus, it is an idol. "The thing" or desire is held more prominently in your consciousness and vision than is Jesus, and your answer will come back tainted. God will give you an answer as delusive as the idol you are entertaining in your heart. He may answer your prayer and give you what you want, but you will later regret it. The children of Israel grumbled, and the Lord gave them what they wanted, but they later regretted it. They ate quail until it almost made them gag!

False peace

You must also beware of false peace. When you have a strong desire to do something, it can produce a false peace that actually comes from your enthusiasm. As time passes, this false peace disappears, and God's true will begins to emerge for your life.

For this reason you should never move too quickly on important decisions. The Bible tells us, "It is dangerous and sinful to rush into the unknown."[6] It is amazing how we can change our minds if we just sit on what we are feeling for a few hours.

Refusing to forgive

We must forgive others who have hurt us in order to hear from God clearly. Additionally, we must stay offense-free. We find an important scriptural key to staying offense-free in Matthew 6:14-15. "For if you forgive men when they sin against you, your heavenly Father will also forgive you. But if you do not forgive men their sins, your Father will not forgive your sins." This is important! *We must forgive those who have hurt us in order to hear the voice of the Lord clearly.*

In Matthew 18, Jesus tells a parable about a man who owed his king one million dollars. He begged the king for mercy and the king had pity on him and canceled the whole debt. The man then went out and found one of his fellow servants who owed him two thousand dollars. He grabbed him by the throat and demanded immediate payment. The fellow servant could not pay so the man had him thrown into prison.

The king discovered what had happened and subsequently had the first man thrown into prison for not showing forgiveness to another. In this parable Jesus was saying that if we don't forgive someone who has hurt us or "ripped us off," we will be delivered to the *torturers* or *demons of hell*.[7]

Even Christians at times can be tormented with confusion, frustration, depression and other disturbances brought on by the demons of hell because they choose not to forgive. Unforgiveness leaves the door wide open for the devil!

We may not feel like forgiving, but because God forgave us, we are commanded to forgive others. God will bring emotional healing into our lives as we obey His Word and forgive in faith from our hearts.

Forgiving does not mean that what they have done to us was right, but it will set us free to hear His voice. The Lord wants to heal us and set us free.

Corrie ten Boom, who experienced life in a Nazi concentration camp, often spoke about "the ding-dong theory." A church bell starts very loud and then grows softer and softer until it finally stops ringing. Corrie said that when you ask the Lord to heal you, the devil may try to bring some of those old emotions of hurt and pain back to you again and again. That is the time for you to say emphatically, "In Jesus' name, I know He took my pain on the cross."

As you declare the truth, the emotions of hurt feelings will dissipate as you focus on Jesus, your healer, instead of on the pain. In the same way that the sound from the big church bell rings loudly at first and then less and less, the memories of hurt will diminish as you declare the truth that Jesus has healed you. In a very short time, you will get to the place where the devil cannot even tempt you any more in this area. You will be completely and totally healed.

In parts of Africa, monkeys are trapped by using a wire cage with just enough room for the monkey to slip his hand inside to pick up a banana that is being used as bait. When the monkey grabs the banana, he cannot get his hand out of the cage because his fist is too large.

All he would need to do is drop the banana, and he would be free; but because he refuses to relinquish the banana, the trappers easily capture the monkey. The moral of the story is to drop your banana (offense) before the devil picks you up and places you in his spiritual, emotional and mental prison.

Hearing God

The Bible speaks of a highway of holiness on which we are to walk, and that "whoever walks the road, although a fool, shall not go astray."[8] Let's learn to stay pure and offense-free in our thoughts and life-styles so we do not fall for the schemes of the enemy that will keep us from hearing the Lord's voice clearly.

Beware the Enemy's Schemes

Verse to remember "For the time will come when men will not put up with sound doctrine. Instead, to suit their own desires, they will gather around them a great number of teachers to say what their itching ears want to hear. They will turn their ears away from the truth and turn aside to myths" (2 Timothy 4:3-4).

Apply what you've learned
1. What are some counterfeits of the Holy Spirit's work?
2. Name some of the devil's schemes to distract you from hearing God's voice.
3. How do we stay "offense free"?

Chapter Twentynine

Becoming God's Friend

I have called you friends, for everything that I heard from
my Father, I have made known to you. John 15:15

Being a friend requires an intimate knowledge of one another.

If two people are best friends, a day does not pass without one friend wanting to talk with the other. Their intimate relationship grew that way because they spent time together sharing their hearts and being honest with each other.

To grow close to God, you have to talk daily! God wants to get to know you and speak to you "face to face" just as He did with Moses. "So the Lord spoke to Moses face to face, as a man speaks to his friend."[1]

Friendship requires love. God loves you! He has lavished His love upon you! That's why He gave the sacrifice of His Son: "All this is done by God, who through Christ changed us from enemies into his friends."[2]

All three persons of the Trinity—God the Father, Son and Holy Spirit—desire friendship and relationship with you and are committed to helping you hear the voice of the Lord clearly.

The Holy Spirit is our guide and friend

Just before Jesus left this earth, He promised His disciples that He would send the Holy Spirit to compensate for the loss of His personal, physical presence in their lives: "I have much more to say to you, more than you can now bear. But when he, the Spirit of truth, comes, he will guide you into all truth. He will not speak on his own; he will speak only what he hears, and he will tell you what is yet to come.[3]

Just as was promised, the Holy Spirit came to be our guide and closest friend. He came to help us discover the Truth and hear from God clearly.

When our family takes a vacation, we sometimes hire a guide to show us the most important sights to see. Some people would rather sight-see by themselves; that way they can explore whatever and whenever they want to. They may find their independent trips wasted though because they spend a large part of the day getting lost and then trying to find their way again.

We've discovered this by experience, so that's why we find the best use of our time comes from following a guide rather than wandering aimlessly! In addition, before planning a trip, I go to the American Automobile Association (AAA) and get expert advice and guidance on the trip.

I believe the Holy Spirit wants to be our AAA guide as we trust Him to guide us into all truth. Our God knew we would need help in understanding His plan for us, so He sent the Holy Spirit to live inside each believer in Jesus Christ. The Bible tells us that the Holy Spirit will never leave us or forsake us, and He is our Guide, our Teacher of Truth, our Counselor, and our Helper. He is also our Comforter or the *parakletos*, one who is "called to one's side" much like an advocate who pleads another's cause (an intercessor)."[4]

The Holy Spirit guides us and ministers truth to us by revelation, not by us trying to figure it out. Jesus told Peter, "On this rock (of revelation) I will build my church."[5]

God's Word encourages every Christian to learn to pray in the Spirit. "But you, dear friends, build yourselves up in your most holy faith and pray in the Holy Spirit."[6]

I personally became more sensitive to hearing the voice of God after I was filled with the Holy Spirit. When I was filled with the Holy Spirit, I experienced a whole new ability to commune with the Holy Spirit and listen to Him speak. In my book "New Testament Baptisms" I write:

> Although I loved the Lord and was part of a youth ministry, I realized there was something missing in my life. I needed the power of the Holy Spirit. I sometimes attended Christian meetings where people were set free from drugs or other life-controlling problems, and I realized these people had a spiritual power that I didn't have.
>
> After studying the scripture and being convinced this experience was based on the Word of God, I humbled myself and went to a pastor who laid his hands on me and prayed for me. That night I was filled with the Holy Spirit.
>
> After I was filled with the Holy Spirit, my life immediately took on a whole new dimension of power. It wasn't me—it was God—the Holy Spirit gave me an intense desire to please Him. Before I was filled with the Holy Spirit, I was involved in a ministry where a few people had given their lives to the Lord. However, after I was filled with the Holy Spirit, everything seemed to change. Hundreds of young people gave their lives to Christ during the next few years. I knew that it certainly wasn't anything that I was doing in my own power and strength. It was the Holy Spirit's power.[7]

If you filled a lantern with oil, you would still have to strike a match and light the lantern so its power could be released. The same principle applies to the truth of the Holy Spirit. I had the Holy Spirit living within me because I had given my life to Christ,[8] but being filled with the Holy Spirit ignited His power in my life.

Although it took me several years from the time I was saved to the time I was filled with the Holy Spirit, I believe it is God's will that we are born again and immediately receive the fullness of the Holy Spirit and the power of God in our lives. The fullness of the Holy Spirit was not just for those at Pentecost, but for all who would believe in Christ throughout this age... "and you will receive the gift of the Holy Spirit. The promise is for you and your children and for all who are far off...."[9]

D. L. Moody, Andrew Murray and many of the other fathers in the faith who were friends of God have testified of the supernatural work of the Holy Spirit in their lives. The same Holy Spirit desires to fill us with His power and teach us to walk in friendship with our God.

God gives specialized direction to each of His children

All who have given their lives to Jesus Christ are called into friendship with God; however, God may require something of us that He does not require of others. For example, Jesus told Peter how he would have to die, and Peter looked at John and said, "What about him?"

Jesus replied, "If I want him to remain alive until I return, what is that to you? You must follow me."[10] We cannot compare what the Lord speaks to us with what He speaks to others.

There are certain things that might be okay for one person but not be right for another. For example, some people believe God wants them to send their children to public school and others believe God has spoken to send their children to private school. Still others believe God has called them to home-school their children. This is why we each need individual direction from God. We should not assume that others are to do things exactly like God has shown us. If we do, we push others toward legalism and dead religion.

God's Word exhorts us to:

> Accept him whose faith is weak, without passing judgment on disputable matters...Who are you to judge someone else's servant? To his own master he stands or falls. And he will stand, for the Lord is able to make him stand. One man considers one day more sacred than another; another man considers every day alike. Each one should be fully convinced in his own mind.[11]

Paul instructed the early Christians to stop passing judgment on the convictions of others. Instead we should accept them because God has accepted them. Christians often differ over matters of conscience. Two Christians may disagree over whether a Christian should eat only vegetables or work on Sundays. These disagreements are not over moral absolutes or doctrines of faith. No two Christians should differ over the doctrinal certainties of the virgin birth or deity of Christ or the moral absolutes of not stealing or lying; however, we can agree to disagree over matters of conscience. We are to accept our fellow Christians where they are in their walk of faith as they learn to hear God's voice for themselves.

Friendship with God requires that we learn to be attentive and sensitive toward hearing from God. Friendship with God places us in a position to welcome the transforming power of God's Spirit in our lives.

The truth is that when God speaks to us, it is completely because of His grace. We are totally dependent upon God's love and grace to be His friend and to hear His voice.

Becoming God's friend

Verse to remember: "I have called you friends..." (John 15:15).

Apply what you've learned

1. Name some attributes of friendship.
2. How has the Lord given you specialized direction?
3. How have you cultivated your friendship with the Lord?

Chapter Thirty

The Adventure of Walking with God

God walked with Adam and Eve in the Garden of Eden, and He has been walking and talking to His people ever since.

The Christian life is frequently called a walk, and believers are exhorted to "walk circumspectly, not as fools but as wise."[1] In fact, Jesus called Himself "the Way,"[2] thereby underlining the journeying nature of our relationship with Him.

To walk before God is to lead a life of devotion to Him. We all know what it is for two friends to walk together, engaged in close and intimate conversation. Having a devoted relationship with someone is an adventure which is full of surprises.

The Bible singles out one of two men in particular by saying, "Enoch walked with God."[3] (The only other man in the entire Bible to also hold this distinction is Noah.) What did Enoch do that placed him in this exclusive God-recognized Hall of Fame?

We know little about Enoch, other than the fact that he lived for 365 years, bore Methuselah and was then translated from life to heaven, thus passing over death. Apparently God honored him because he walked pleasingly before the Lord. He was an individual who realized he was always under the seeing eye of God. His life was a life of communion with God.

Trust God's higher ways

My wife LaVerne and I talk to our children all the time as do most parents. Why wouldn't our heavenly Father desire to talk to His children? The truth of the matter is that we would not expect our children to know what we wanted them to do if we did not talk to them. So then, why would God feel any differently?

We have to be willing to trust God and have faith in Him even when we do not understand His ways. Sometimes we do not know the meaning of what God says until we look back later in life.

The way God thinks is far beyond the way we think. "As the heavens are higher than the earth, so are my ways higher than your ways and my thoughts than your thoughts."[4] Even if God's thoughts surpass ours, and we do not always understand His ways, God wants us to get to know His ways! That's why we should intentionally listen for His voice.

A husband may be relaxing and feel impressed to help his wife with some of the maintenance around the house. He should not be too quick to rebuke that thought! It is probably the Lord speaking to him. A teenager listening to her favorite CD or talking to one of her friends on the telephone may hear a voice within telling her to clean her room. It is probably God speaking!

Practice and obey

We learn to hear the voice of the Lord through practice and obedience. Sometimes we may feel discouraged trying to discern between the Lord's voice, the enemy's voice, others' voices, and our own voices. Sometimes it may seem like we are listening to a radio station with a weak signal, while a few other stations continue to fade in and out; but, as we continue to listen to the voice of our Shepherd, we will learn the difference between the voices.

Years ago, we were at a shopping mall with our two younger children. In one split second our then four-year-old daughter was missing from view. I instantly called out her name. Thankfully, she quickly responded to the voice of her father. I was so relieved to see her! Our heavenly Father wants His children to heed His voice. *Lord, teach us to hear Your voice and obey it.*

Take steps of faith

When I read in Acts that Paul and Silas were trying to go into Bithynia and were being prevented by the Spirit, it was life changing for me. Without knowing the full scope of God's plan, they obeyed the Spirit's voice and went in another direction. It turned out that the Holy Spirit had greater plans for Paul and Silas that they did not recognize at the time.

Taking this biblical example, I was no longer afraid to take steps of faith. I knew I could trust the Lord to keep me from going places that were not in His perfect plan for me. I could trust Him to lead me with His divine direction and in faith step out into God's plans.

When I was a teenager and met the girl I thought was to be my wife, I told God every day for nearly three years, "Please speak to me clearly if she is the one I should marry." I knew I wanted to marry her, but I had to be sure that God was also speaking this to us both.

Some of God's people spend their lives in so much fear of making a mistake that they never do anything. There are times when it is much better to do something, rather than continue to do nothing. Without faith it is impossible to please God. We cannot trust in our own abilities but we can trust in His ability because Christ lives in us.

Jesus honored whatever His Father said, no matter what the personal cost, and it cost Him His life. We will not hear the Lord's voice clearly if we only listen to God when what He says is not going to cost us anything, or if we only listen when He tells us what we want to hear.

We must be willing to lay aside our own desires or we may miss a clear word from the Lord. Our natural inclination tends to manipulate things to work the way we want them to work.

We need to be open to messages God may send through people who love us and are praying for us. God wants us to stay humble and always be ready to hear from Him whichever way He chooses to speak.

Learning to hear is a process

We can learn some valuable insights on hearing from God from George Mueller, a man of faith from 19th-century England. Here are some of his suggestions:

> I seek at the beginning to get my heart in such a state that it has no will of its own in regard to a given matter....Nine-tenths of the difficulties are overcome when our hearts are ready to do the Lord's will whatever it may be...Having done this, I do not leave the result to feeling or simple impression. If so, I make myself liable to great delusions. I will seek the will of the Spirit of God through, or in connection with, the Word of God....If the Holy Ghost guides us at all, He will do it according to the scriptures and never contrary to them...Next, I take into account providential circumstances. These often plainly indicate God's will in connection with His Word and Spirit. I ask God in prayer to reveal His will to me aright...Thus, through prayer to God, the study of the Word, and reflection, I come to deliberate judgment according to the best of my ability and knowledge, and if my mind is thus at peace, and continues so after two or three more petitions, I proceed accordingly. In trivial matters and in transactions involving most important issues, I find this method effective...[5]

> But if honesty of heart and uprightness before God were lacking, or if I did not patiently wait upon God

for instruction, or if I preferred the counsel of my fellow man to the declarations of the Word of the living God, I made great mistakes.[6]

Even after many years of practicing God's presence, Mr. Muller admitted that he still made mistakes in hearing from God. There is no fool-proof method to hearing.

Live in expectancy: expect to hear from God!

The psalmist directed his prayers to God expecting an answer, "In the morning I lay my requests before you and wait in expectation."[7] God wants us to make our first petitions to Him each day as we live in expectancy of an answer. Jeremiah 33:3 says, "Call unto me and I will answer you and show you great and mighty things...." When we seek God, He promises to answer—of that we can be sure.

Loren Cunningham, the founder of Youth With A Mission, says that he has found three simple steps that have helped him and thousands of others to hear God's voice:

SUBMIT to His Lordship. Ask Him to help you silence your own thoughts, desires, and the opinions of others which may be filling your mind.[8] Even though you have been given a good mind to use, you want to hear the thoughts of the Lord who has the best mind.[9]

RESIST the enemy in case he is trying to deceive you. Use the authority that Jesus Christ has given you to silence the voice of the enemy.[10]

EXPECT an answer. After asking the question that is on your mind, wait for Him to answer. Expect your loving heavenly father to speak to you, and He will.[11]

Hearing from God is a journey. After many years of listening for His voice, I still sometimes make mistakes in hearing clearly. But I am learning, and you will too! Just as a young baby quickly learns to know his daddy's voice, and responds to it by turning toward that loving, familiar voice, you will learn to hear God's voice as you love Him and obey Him.

My prayer for you is that you will experience the Lord and hear His voice in a whole new dimension as you continue your lifetime walk with Jesus. Let's together fulfill the Lord's purpose for our lives as we look forward to His return. May the Lord bless you richly as you listen to the Lord speak to you and experience the joy of obeying His voice.

Your fellow servant in Christ,
Larry Kreider

The adventure of walking with God

Verse to remember:
"See then that you walk circumspectly..."
(Ephesians 5:15 NKJV).

Apply what you've learned
1. How is your walk with God a journey?
2. How does the Lord keep you from going places that are not in His perfect plan for you?
3. Describe a time you broke through and took a step of faith in hearing from God.

Notes

Introduction
1 Job 33:14
2 Mark 4:24 (AMP)
3 John 10:5 (AMP)
4 John 3:1-21
5 2 Corinthians 5:5
6 1 Corinthians 2:11
7 C. S. Lewis, *The Chronicles of Narnia*, (New York: Macmillan Publishing Company, 1950), Mr. Beaver warning the children about Aslan.

Chapter 1: Tuning in to God
1 John 10:4
2 Jeremiah 33:3
3 Larry Kreider, *House to House,* (Ephrata, PA: House to House Publications, 1995), p.1
4 Jeremiah 29:12-13
5 Matthew 7:7; Luke 11:9; Revelation 3:20
6 Proverbs 3:5-6
7 Luke 24:13-32
8 Genesis 3:8

Chapter 2: Hearing the Right Voice
1 Hebrews 11:6
2 2 Corinthians 10:5
3 2 Corinthians 11:14
4 Matthew 4:4 (TEV)
5 James 4:7-8
6 1 John 4:4
7 1 Samuel 3:1-12
8 Hebrews 5:14 (CEV)
9 John 8:31-32 (NASB)

Chapter 3: The Bible
1 John 6:63
2 Matthew 4:4
3 2 Timothy 2:15 (AMP)
4 2 Corinthians 6:14
5 2 Timothy 3:16-17
6 Mark 10:11-12
7 Steve Prokopchak, *In Pursuit of Obedience,* (Ephrata, PA: House to House Publications, 2002) p. 10
8 Ephesians 2:8-9
9 Philippians 2:12
10 Daniel B. Wallace, "Scripture Twisting!" www.Bible.org, 2004.
11 1 Corinthians 14:37
12 Galatians 1:6-8
13 2 Corinthians 11:14
14 Acts 17:10-12
15 Luke 5:34
16 Hebrews 4:12
17 Proverbs 4:20-21 (AMP)

Chapter 4: His Peace
1 Joshua 1:8
2 John 14:27
3 Philippians 4:7
4 Colossians 3:15
5 Philippians 4:7
6 Joyce Meyer, *How to Hear From God,* (Time Warner Book Group, 2003), p. 85.

Chapter 5: Circumstances
1 Revelation 3:7 (AMP)
2 1 Corinthians 16:5-9 (NIV)
3 1 Corinthians 13:9
4 Jeremiah 32:6-8 (LB)
5 Joyce Meyer, *How to Hear From God,* (Time Warner Book Group, 2003), p. 176.

Chapter 6: His Still, Small Voice
1 1 Kings 19:11-13 (Amplified Bible)
2 Mark Virkler, *Communion With God,* (Elma, New York), www.cwgministries.org
3 Romans 8:16
4 Proverbs 20:27
5 Proverbs 16:9
6 John 10:4

Chapter 7: People
1 Proverbs 11:14 (NKJV)
2 Proverbs 15:23
3 2 Corinthians 13:1
4 Matthew 18:19-20
5 Romans 10:14
6 John Stott, *Between Two Worlds,* (Grand Rapids, Michigan: Wm. B. Eerdmans Publishing Co, 1982, Reprinted 2000) pp. 15-16.
7 Proverbs 15:22
8 1 John 4:1
9 1 Thessalonians 5:12 (AMP)
10 Matthew 7:15-20

Chapter 8: Common Sense Wisdom
1 James 1:5
2 Proverbs 3:13 (LB)
3 Proverbs 3:21-22 (LB)

[4] Proverbs 4:5 (LB)
[5] Proverbs 4:7 (LB)
[6] Proverbs 10:13 (LB)
[7] Proverbs 10:21 (LB)
[8] Proverbs 14:6 (LB)
[9] Proverbs 14:33 (LB)
[10] Proverbs 16:21 (LB)
[11] Psalm 119:124-125 (LB)
[12] Proverbs 3:3-4 (LB)
[13] Proverbs 17:10 (LB)
[14] Proverbs 21:16 (LB)
[15] Proverbs 24:3 (LB)
[16] 1 Corinthians 6:2-3

Chapter 9: Conviction

[1] John 16:7-10
[2] Oswald Chambers, *My Utmost for His Highest*, (Oswald Chambers Publications Association Ltd., Updated Edition in Today's Language, 1992), December 7.
[3] Ezekiel 36:26
[4] 1 Corinthians 10:13
[5] Hebrews 4:16

Chapter 10: Worship

[1] Psalm 147:11 (CEV)
[2] Luke 7:36-50
[3] Rick Warren, *The Purpose Driven Life* (Grand Rapids, Michigan: Zondervan, 2002), 67
[4] 1 Corinthians 10:31
[5] John 4:24
[6] Psalms 22:3
[7] Donald E. Demaray, *Alive to God Through Prayer* (Grand Rapids: Baker Book House, 1965), 27.
[8] 1 Thessalonians 5:18 (RSV)
[9] 1 Thessalonians 5:19 (RSV)
[10] Philippians 2:14-15
[11] John 15:7 (AMP)

Chapter 11: Authorities

[1] Matthew 28:18 (NKJV)
[2] 1 Peter 2:13 (RSV)
[3] Romans 13:1-2
[4] Isaiah 14:14 (NKJV)
[5] Jeremiah 23:29
[6] John 5:30
[7] Acts 5:29
[8] Daniel 1:8,12-13
[9] Nehemiah 1

Chapter 12: Natural Things

[1] Psalm 29:3-9
[2] Genesis 15:5
[3] Romans 1:20
[4] Romans 1:21
[5] Whittaker Chambers, *Witness*, (Regnery Publishing; Reissue edition, 1987), p. 15
[6] Matthew 6:28
[7] Luke 12:24
[8] Mark 4:26-29
[9] Matthew 16:2-3
[10] Matthew 24:32-33
[11] Exodus 13:21-22
[12] Exodus 40:34-35
[13] 1 Kings 8:11-13

Chapter 13: The Church

[1] Hebrews 3:13
[2] Matthew 16:18
[3] Ephesians 3:14-15
[4] 1 Corinthians 10:13
[5] Hebrews 13:7,17
[6] 1 Peter 5:8
[7] 1 Thessalonians 5:12-13

Chapter 14: His Character

[1] John 3:16
[2] 1 John 4:7-8
[3] Psalm 103:7 (NKJV)
[4] Psalm 103:3-4 (NKJV)
[5] Galatians 2:20
[6] John 1:1
[7] Matthew 17:5
[8] Dwight Edwards, *Revolution Within*, (Colorado Springs, CO: WaterBook Press, 2001), p.58.
[9] John 10:10 (NKJV)
[10] John 10:30
[11] John 8:28
[12] Psalm 20:4; Psalm 37:4

Chapter 15: Visions and Dreams

[1] Acts 2:17
[2] Job 33:14-17 (NLT)
[3] 2 Corinthians 12:1-4
[4] 1 John 4:1-3
[5] Genesis 40 and 41
[6] Matthew 1 and 2
[7] Matthew 2:19-23
[8] Joyce Meyer, *How to Hear From God*, (Time Warner Book Group, 2003), p. 49.

Book recommendation: *Your Dreams; God's Neglected Gift* by Herman Riffel.

Chapter 16: Various Spiritual Gifts

1 Romans 1:11-12
2 1 Corinthians 12:7-11
3 Acts 16:16-18
4 For more about speaking in tongues: Read Larry Kreider's Biblical Foundation Series: book # 3, *New Testament Baptisms* (Lititz, PA: House to House Publications, 2002).
5 Acts 2:4-12
6 Jack Hayford, *The Beauty of Spiritual Language,* (Dallas: Word Publishing, 1992).
7 Ibid., p. 199-200.
8 1 Corinthians 14:1

Chapter 17: Prophecy

1 1 Corinthians 14:3
2 Dr. Bill Hamon, *Prophets and Personal Prophecy* (Shippensburg, PA: Destiny Image, 1987), p. 29
3 Acts 21 and 22
4 1 Timothy 4:14
5 1 Timothy 1:18
6 1 Thessalonians 5:19-22
7 John 21:23
8 Luke 21:15

Chapter 18: A Daily Encounter

1 Max Lucado, *Just Like Jesus,* (Nashville: Word Publishing, 1998), 45.
2 Ralph W. Neighbour, Jr., *The Arrival Kit,* (Houston, TX: Touch Publications, 1993), p. 62.
3 Song of Solomon 2:10
4 You can access this "Bible reading plan" by visiting our ministry's Web site at www.dcfi.org.
5 Mark 1:35
6 Luke 5:16

Chapter 19: Journaling

1 Proverbs 7:1-3
2 Habakkuk 2:1-3
3 *Communion With God,* Mark & Patti Virkler, (Orchard Park, New York: Buffalo School of the Bible, 1986), p. 29.

Chapter 20: Prayer and Fasting

Many thanks to my friend and associate, Brian Sauder, for his insights for this chapter.
1 Cornell Haan, "Which Intercessor Most Influenced Your Prayer Life? *Charisma Magazine,* September/October 2004, p. 14.
2 Acts 10:30-32
3 Luke 1:11-13
4 Luke 11:5-13
5 James 4:2
6 James 4:8
7 Luke 18
8 Mark 9:29 (NKJV)
9 *The Full Life Study Bible,* General Editor Donald Stamps, (Grand Rapids, MI: Zondervan Publishing House, 1992).
10 Matthew 6:16
11 Acts 13:3
12 Acts 14:23
13 Daniel 10:12
14 **Recommended book on fasting:** Bill Bright, *The Transforming Power of Fasting & Prayer* (New Life Publications).

Chapter 21: Angels

1 Hebrews 1:14 (LB)
2 Billy Graham, *Angels,* (Dallas, TX: Word Publishing, 1986), p. 61.
3 Galatians 1:8
4 2 Corinthians 11:14
5 Paul Kengor, *God and Ronald Reagan,* (Regan Books, 2004), p. 186.
6 Acts 12:7-15
7 Matthew 18:10 (LB)
8 Hebrews 13:2
9 Billy Graham, *Angels,* (Dallas, TX: Word Publishing, 1986), p. 3.

Chapter 22: Surprises

1 Numbers 22:21-34
2 Matthew 3:17
3 John 12:29
4 2 Chronicles 35:20-24
5 Isaiah 30:21(NAS)
6 Oswald Chambers, *My Utmost for His Highest,* (Grand Rapids, Michigan: Discovery House, 1992), March 29.

Chapter 23: The Unique Way He Made Us

Many thanks to my friend Marcelo Almeida from Sao Paulo, Brazil, for insights for this chapter taken from his book entitled *The Anointing and the Prophetic Purpose* by Marcelo Almeida, 2000.

1. Proverbs 22:6
2. Jeremiah 1:5
3. Romans 12:3-8

Chapter 24: Signs

1. Judges 6:36-40
2. Genesis 9:12-15
3. Joshua 10:12-14

Chapter 25: Practicing His Presence

1. Max Lucado, *Just Like Jesus,* (Nashville: Word Publishing, 1998), 59.
2. Psalm 46:10
3. Brother Lawrence, *The Practice of the Presence of God,* (New Kensington, PA: Whitaker House, 1982), p.49, 80.
4. Ibid., p. 24, 80.
5. 1 Thessalonians 5:17
6. Joyce Meyer, *How to Hear From God,* (Time Warner Book Group, 2003), p. 15.
7. Psalm 37:23-24 (NKJV)

Chapter 26: His Silence

1. Oswald Chambers, *My Utmost For His Highest,* (Michigan: Discovery House, 1992).
2. Psalm 66:18 (NLT)
3. 1 Samuel 3:1
4. 2 Kings 6:1-6
5. Joel 2:25 (NKJV)
6. Revelation 2:5
7. Isaiah 30:15,18 (RSV)
8. Zephaniah 3:17 (NAS)
9. Paul Thigpen, "O God, Do Not Be Silent," Charisma Magazine, April 1992, p.59.
10. Psalm 139:7, 9-10
11. Hebrews 13:5

Chapter 27: Partial Revelation

1. 1 Corinthians 13:9
2. Proverbs 16:9 (RSV)
3. Matthew 2:19-23
4. Acts 16
5. Hebrews 11:1
6. 1 Corinthians 2:13-15
7. 1 Corinthians 2:16b
8. Romans 8:28 (NKJV)

9. 2 Timothy 2:24 (KJV)
10. 1 Chronicles 14

Chapter 28: Beware the Enemy's Schemes

1. 2 Timothy 4:3-4
2. Leviticus 19:31
3. *Devotional Classics,* edited by Foster and Smith, (San Francisco, CA, Harper, 1990), p. 9.
4. Psalm 66:18
5. Ezekiel 14:1-5
6. Proverbs 19.2
7. Matthew 18:34-35
8. Isaiah 35:8

Chapter 29: Becoming God's Friend

1. Exodus 33:11 (NKJV)
2. 2 Corinthians 5:18 (TEV)
3. John 16:12-14
4. W. E. Vine, Merrill F. Unger, William White Jr., *Vine's Complete Expository Dictionary of Old and New Testament Words* (Nashville: Thomas Nelson, Inc., 1984, 1996), p. 111.
5. Matthew 16:18
6. Jude 20
7. Larry Kreider, *New Testament Baptisms,* (Ephrata, PA: House to House Publications, 2002), p.32.
8. Romans 8:9
9. Acts 2:38-39
10. John 21:19-22
11. Romans 14:1,4-5

Chapter 30: The Adventure of Walking With God

1. Ephesians 5:15 (NKJV)
2. John 14:6
3. Genesis 5:24
4. Isaiah 55:9
5. *Answers to Prayer from George Mueller's Narratives,* compiled by A.E.C. Brooks.
6. From the classic biography of George Mueller, *George Mueller of Bristol,* by A. T. Pierson.
7. Psalm 5:3
8. 2 Corinthians 10:5
9. Proverbs 3:5-6
10. James 4:7; Ephesians 6:10-20
11. John 10:27; Psalms 69:13; Exodus 33:11

Serving Jesus Christ as Lord

The place to start your journey of hearing from God is by making sure you have a personal relationship with Jesus Christ. Sitting in a church service won't make you a Christian any more than sitting in a garage will make you a car! In Matthew 7:23, the Bible states that there are people who will say at the judgment day, "Lord, Lord, we have done many mighty works in Your name," and He will say to them, "I never knew you; depart from Me, you who act wickedly." To some people, Christianity is based on their outward appearance or on what they do rather than a real love for the Lord. They appear righteous outwardly, but inwardly they are not born of God and the Spirit. Jesus sternly reprimanded the Pharisees and scribes in Mark 7:6 for this kind of hypocrisy. ...*These people honor me with their lips, but their hearts are far from me.*

For years, I was in the same league as the Pharisees. I considered myself a Christian, but I was living a counterfeit Christian life. My family attended church every Sunday during my childhood. When I was eleven years old, we went to a special evangelistic meeting. I really didn't want to go to hell so I stood up when the evangelist gave an "altar call." I was later water baptized to become part of the church.

My commitment to the Lord was incomplete, so it wasn't long before I was living a fake Christian life. I only acted like a Christian when I was with my Christian friends. (This is also called "hypocrisy.) Seven years later, a friend confronted me: "If you were to die tonight, are you sure you would go to heaven?" I honestly didn't know the answer, so I said, "Nobody knows that."

The young lady didn't hesitate with her answer. She said, "Well, I know."

I had come face to face with the truth. Sure, I could talk about God and the Bible; however, I couldn't talk about *Jesus* because I didn't *know* Him in a personal way. I had made an initial commitment to the Lord, but I believed that somehow God would accept me if I did enough good things along the way. I didn't realize that eternal life comes only through faith in Jesus *Christ as Lord.*

Later that night, when I opened my Bible at home, everything seemed to be written directly to me. I read where Jesus said, "You hypocrites!" and I knew I was a hypocrite too. My friends considered me to be "the life of the party," but I knew the truth. Loneliness was my companion every evening that I spent at home alone. Even worse, I was afraid that if I died in the night, I would die without God for eternity. I came to the realization I was under a counterfeit conversion. That night I said, "Jesus, I give You my life. If You can use this rotten, mixed-up life, I'll serve You the rest of my life."

God miraculously changed me the moment I reached out in faith to Him. My attitudes and desires changed. Even my thinking began to change. This time, I knew I was clearly born again because Jesus Christ had become my *Lord.* I was a new creation in Christ, and I am eternally grateful to Jesus.

If you are trying to appear righteous but continue to pursue sinful directions in your heart and mind, you may be living a counterfeit Christian life. Now is the time to ask the Holy Spirit to shine God's light on your heart. Come to the cross of Jesus, confess your sin and accept God's forgiveness. God might be speaking to you right now.

If you are not sure you have been born again, if you have never acknowledged Jesus as the Lord of your life, if you need to recommit your life to Jesus Christ, if you desire to have an intimate relationship with Him, wait no longer. Today is your day. Today you can begin to hear His voice clearly.

Pray this prayer of confession and repentance and receive God's unconditional love and forgiveness. *Lord, I have been trapped in the web of hypocrisy and long for the freedom I can have in You. I confess that I have tried to be righteous without You and I confess my sin to You. Please forgive my sin so I can come under the power and control and influence of Your righteousness. Thank You for setting me free, Jesus. I pray for courage and wisdom to live out my new life in Christ and experience the fullness and freedom You desire for me to have. I ask this all in Jesus' name. Amen.*

30 of the Many Ways God Speaks

God is speaking. Are you listening? Allow the Lord to speak to you in any way that He chooses, including these 30 ways. Consider taking 30 days to learn to listen—one day for each way.

God speaks through:

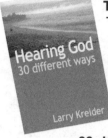
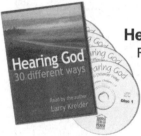

Other books by Larry Kreider

Biblical Foundation Series

This series by Larry Kreider covers basic Christian doctrine. Practical illustrations accompany the easy-to-understand format. Use for small group teachings (48 in all), a mentoring relationship or daily devotional. Each book has 64 pages: **$4.99** each, includes these titles:

1. Knowing Jesus Christ as Lord
2. The New Way of Living
3. New Testament Baptisms
4. Building For Eternity
5. Living in the Grace of God
6. Freedom from the Curse
7. Learning to Fellowship with God
8. What is the Church?
9. Authority and Accountability
10. God's Perspective on Finances
11. Called to Minister
12. The Great Commission

Save on a complete 12 Book Set: **$39**

Biblical Foundations for Children

Creative learning experiences for ages 4-12, patterned after the Biblical Foundation Series. Takes kids on the first steps in their Christian walk. By Jane Nicholas, 176 pages: **$17.95**

The Cry for Spiritual Fathers & Mothers

The Book Returning to the biblical truth of spiritual parenting so believers are not left fatherless and disconnected. How loving, seasoned spiritual fathers and mothers help spiritual children reach their full potential in Christ. *by Larry Kreider, 186 pages:* **$11.95**

Audio Set of six topics. *Six Tape or CD Set:* **$29.00**

Group Video Training Complete set includes six or twelve sessions for all sizes of group training. Set of three video tapes in a protective binder, a *Leader's Guide,* six *Participant Manuals*, and a copy of the book *The Cry for Spiritual Fathers & Mothers*: **$99.00**

Call 800.848.5892
www.dcfi.org   email: info@dcfi.org

House to House

The church is waking up to the simple, successful house to house strategy practiced by the New Testament church. *House to House* documents how God called a small fellowship of believers to become a house to house movement. During the past years, DOVE Christian Fellowship Int'l has grown into a family of cell-based churches and house churches networking throughout the world. *by Larry Kreider, 206 pages:* **$8.95**

Elders for Today's Church

Healthy leadership teams produce healthy churches! New Testament principles for equipping church leadership teams: Why leadership is needed, what their qualifications and responsibilities are, how they should be chosen, how elders function as spiritual fathers and mothers, how they are to make decisions, resolve conflicts, and more. Included are questionnaires for evaluating a team of elders. *By Larry Kreider, Ron Myer, Steve Prokopchak, and Brian Sauder, 274 pages:* **$12.99**

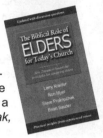

Elders Audio Set

Included in this series are the New Testament leadership principles to train elders to provide protection, direction and correction in the local church. *Six Tape or CD Set includes twelve topics:* **$35.00**

Elders DVD Training

Twelve sessions taught by the four authors of the book! The complete set includes a copy of *The Biblical Role of Elders* book, a leader's guide, three DVDs and six student manuals: **$89**

The Tithe: A Test in Trust

This book answers key questions about tithing based on the scriptures, explaining it as both an Old Testament and a New Testament teaching. Written with a variety of illustrations, this book has been used to help believers understand that the tithe is a test in trust—trust in God and trust in our spiritual leadership. *by Larry Kreider. 32 pages:* **$4.99**

House Church Networks

A new model of church is emerging. Discover how these new house church networks offer community and simplicity, especially as they fit the heart, call and passion of the younger generations. These house church networks will work together with the more traditional community churches and mega-churches to show the transforming power of Christ to our neighborhoods. *by Larry Kreider, 118 pages:* **$9.99**

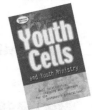

Hearing From God

Learn to "tune in" to God and discern "HIS" voice. God wants to speak to you. Includes a seminar manual.

Spiritual Fathering & Mothering Seminar

Practical preparation for believers who want to have and become spiritual parents. Includes a seminar manual.

Elder's Training Seminar

Based on New Testament leadership principles, this seminar equips leaders to provide protection, direction and correction in the local church. Includes a seminar manual.

Small Groups 101 Seminar

Basics for healthy cell ministry. Session topics cover the essentials for growing cell group ministry. Each attendee receives a *Helping You Build Manual*.

Small Groups 201 Seminar

Takes you beyond the basics and into an advanced strategy for cell ministry. Each attendee receives a seminar manual.

Counseling Basics

This seminar takes you through the basics of counseling, specifically in small group ministry. Includes a comprehensive manual.

Marriage Mentoring Training Seminar

Trains church leaders and mature believers to help prepare engaged couples for a strong marriage foundation by using the mentoring format of *Called Together*. Includes a *Called Together Manual*.

**For additional seminars
and more information
www.dcfi.org
Call 800.848.5892   email: info@dcfi.org**

Notes

Notes